Self-Love Guide for Women

A Complete Workbook to Help you Build Self-Confidence, Self-esteem, Self-Compassion, and Find Genuine Happiness

Natalie Morgon

Table of Contents

Introduction

Congratulations on purchasing this book.

Do you tend to feel confused by your thoughts? Do you want to stop thinking about your life in general and let it flow as it is? Dealing with negative thoughts or feelings is not an easy task. The primary thing you will need to deal with life problems is self-love. Self-love acts as the magic that can mend the course of your life besides making it a lot better. But it is also something that cannot be mastered overnight. If you are someone who does not think about yourself or cannot recognize your worth, developing self-love will take more time.

The aim of this book is to make you aware of self-love and provide you with suggestions and tips that will help you cultivate the same easily. All of us tend to regulate our emotions more than we can actually realize. But if you can understand how to handle your mind, you will be able to open the doors to the immensity of brilliance and imagination. The prime key to leading a dream life is to understand your worth in the first place. As you do so, you will get the clarity of prioritizing important things in life, all those things that serve no purpose, and the way you want to live your life.

There are plenty of books on this subject on the market; thanks again for choosing this one! Every effort was made to ensure it is full of as much useful information as possible. Please enjoy!

Chapter 1: What Is Self-Love?

Self-love might sound great; however, what is it in reality? How can someone love themself, and why does it even matter? Self-love is all about accepting yourself fully and treating yourself with respect and kindness, besides nurturing your well-being and growth. Self-love does not only include the way you treat yourself but also your feelings and thoughts about yourself. So, as you conceptualize self-love, you can imagine what you will do for yourself. You can also try to imagine how you would talk to yourself and how you would feel about yourself, which tends to reflect concern and love.

As you get to love yourself, you can have a positive view of yourself. It does not indicate that you will feel positive about yourself all the time. If you think of it like this, it would be unrealistic.

For instance, you can temporarily feel angry, disappointed, or upset with yourself and still love yourself. If this seems to be confusing for you, try to think of how it functions in other relationships. You can love your partner even when you feel disappointed or angry with him/her at times. Even when you feel disappointed or angry, your love for your partner informs how you relate to him/her. It will let you forgive them, meet their needs, consider their feelings, and also make decisions that can support their well-being. Self-love is more or less the same. If you are aware of how to love other people, you must be aware of how to love yourself.

What Does Self-Love Look Like?

Here are some examples that can help you understand self-love in action.

- Forgiving yourself as you mess up
- Saying positive things to oneself
- Being assertive
- Meeting your requirements
- Asking for help
- Spending time with all those who build you up and support you
- Prioritizing your well-being and health
- Not allowing others to take advantage of you
- Valuing what you feel
- Understanding your strengths
- Letting go of anger or grudges that hold you back
- Challenging yourself
- Living according to your values
- Pursuing your goals and interests
- Accepting your imperfections
- Providing yourself healthy treats
- Holding yourself accountable
- Noticing your effort and progress
- Setting realistic expectations

Why Do You Need to Love Yourself?

If you grew up without any kind of model of self-love or anyone discussing the importance of being good to yourself, you would surely question its value. It is said that when there is no existence of self-love, you are most likely to be self-critical and fall prey to perfectionism and people-pleasing. Also, you will be more likely to tolerate mistreatment or abuse from other people. You might pay no attention to your requirements and feelings as you cannot value yourself. You might make self-sabotage or opt for making decisions that might not be in your best interest. It is believed that self-love acts as the foundation that lets us set boundaries, be assertive, and develop healthy relationships with other people. Additionally, it will let you practice self-care, be proud of who you are, and pursue your goals and interests.

Self-love is also referred to as self-compassion. It also includes taking care of your needs, accepting your failures, weaknesses, and strengths, and being in touch with your emotions. As selflessness is a prized virtue in various circles, there are people who believe it to be egotistical. Caring for others is indeed necessary. However, it should never come at the expense of your well-being. Why? Here are some reasons to clarify the concept.

Reduces stress

Self-care is an essential aspect of self-love. As you love yourself, you can easily recognize the burnout signs and can take the necessary steps to deal with stress. When self-love is not present, you might not be able to understand or believe that you require a break. The very thought of doing anything "for me" might turn out to be quite challenging to accept. So, you are most likely to deal with a stressful time when it hurts.

But on the other hand, people with healthy self-love are always more willing to take out time to love themselves as they get stressed.

Improves emotional resilience

During hard times, one of the easiest things to do is to slip into despair. Based on the environment you are in, you might end up dealing with all those individuals who tend to blame you for the hardships you come across. As a result, you might start blaming yourself. Self-love acts as a powerful weapon in countering critical self-talk and putting everything in proper perspective. Even if the struggles you face result from your mistakes, self-love can always encourage you to learn from your mistakes and move ahead in life. It will help in improving your emotional resilience and make you ready for upcoming challenges.

Build healthier habits

It is said that being able to love yourself can help a lot in making better health decisions. It is also believed that when you start to accept yourself without any kind of harsh judgment, you can get more motivated to make positive changes in your life. Also, self-compassion can always help you to form healthier and new habits.

Improves relationships

You must have heard of the saying that you cannot love other people until you can love yourself. While it might seem a bit extreme, loving yourself can always help you to improve your relationships with other people. As you love yourself, you will no longer feel dependent on others for a sense of worth. It can directly help you to set boundaries or end unhealthy connections if needed. Also, all those who can love themselves can understand themselves much better. It can help you determine the type of relationships you want or do not want.

Reduce depression and anxiety symptoms

It has been found that people who possess high levels of self-compassion tend to have a much lower risk of developing depression or anxiety. But it does not indicate that you are not capable of loving yourself if you are depressed or anxious. All it implies is that the aspects of self-love can help manage or reduce depression and anxiety symptoms. Also, self-love can help you free yourself from the belief mental clutter is all your fault.

Makes you productive

We are all aware of the fact that procrastination is a productivity killer. In order to motivate yourself, you might need to opt for harsh tactics. There are people who end up using threats of self-punishment to try and finish a task. But such things can never be regarded as an effective motivator. If you procrastinate, it will be better for you to have compassion for yourself. You will have to use your failure as a chance to learn new things in the future. In place of being consumed with self-criticism, you can feel a lot lighter and prepare yourself to make behavioral changes.

Increases happiness

Loving and accepting yourself is connected to higher satisfaction in life. So, it can be said that self-love will lead to more happiness in life. When you keep analyzing all your flaws besides criticizing your decisions, it will be hard for you to feel happy regarding anything. But self-love can encourage you to think of yourself like a dear friend. You can understand that you are not perfect but still worthy of support and acceptance.

Helps in achieving goals

Self-love can teach you that your dreams deserve priority. Keep in mind that it is never selfish to go after all that you desire in life. Others might try to tell you that you are being so. However, as long as you are not stamping on other people to attain your goals, you should lead your life the way that fulfills you. Also, self-love can provide you with all those tools that you require to attain your dreams, like emotional resilience, reduced stress, confidence, and enhanced productivity.

Boosts confidence

It can turn out to be quite tough to feel confident if you are concentrated on criticizing yourself. All those who are habituated with negative self-talk often tend to struggle with low self-esteem. With it, a lack of confidence follows naturally. If you desire to feel more confident, self-love is a great way to train that muscle. Try to recognize your skills and worth, be compassionate as you get frustrated with your own self, and you can see your confidence developing.

Inspires others

The overall concept of self-love might be quite challenging. You might build the habit of working through the belief that self-love is all about selfishness. But being able to love yourself can help others. Similar to happiness, self-love also can be contagious. If you can successfully model what a healthy relationship with yourself looks like, it can help others to see why it is so important. They can start to practice more self-compassion and self-care. Every individual around you can benefit when you learn to love yourself.

Self-Love vs. Narcissism

Besides questioning if self-love is really necessary, another huge barrier to self-love is the belief that it is narcissistic. When therapists and psychologists encourage self-love, they never ask you to put yourself on a pedestal right above others. Narcissists tend to believe that they are always better than other people. Also, they will never take responsibility or acknowledge their flaws and mistakes. Also, they seek excessive external recognition and validation. Additionally, narcissists do not tend to have empathy for other people.

On the other hand, self-love has nothing to do with showing off how great someone is. All those who love themselves in a healthy way are aware of the fact that they are flawed. They can understand that they make mistakes, and they care about themselves regardless of their imperfections. Self-love will not prevent you from caring for other people. It is all about giving yourself the same sort of kindness that you tend to give to other people.

Steps to Cultivate Self-Love

Here are some of the steps that can assist you in the cultivation of self-love.

- **Being mindful:** Individuals who are aware of self-love knows about all that they want, think about, and feel. They tend to be quite mindful of the person they are. In fact, they try to always act according to the same knowledge instead of acting on all that other people desire from them.

- **Practice self-care:** You can start loving yourself even more as you can take proper care of the basic requirements of your life. Individuals who are habituated to practicing self-love tend to nourish themselves every day with hearty activities, such as exercise, proper nutrition, enough sleep, healthy social relationships, and intimacy.

- **Act on all that you require instead of all that you want:** Anyone can love themselves the moment they can move away from things that make them feel excited and good to something that they require to stay centered and strong in life. As you concentrate on all that you require, you can maintain distance from patterns of automatic behavior that tend to bring trouble in life. You will be able to move ahead of the past and increase self-care.

- **Set boundaries:** You will be able to provide more love to yourself as you can set boundaries or be able to say "no" to activities, or work that might harm/deplete you physically or emotionally. Also, you will be able to express yourself better.

- **Forgive yourself:** Human beings have the tendency to be hard with themselves. The drawback of trying to take all the responsibilities for your actions is to punish yourself excessively for the missteps in growing and learning. We will need to comply with our humanness before we can truly love ourselves. It is necessary to practice being less hard on yourself as you end up making any mistakes. Keep in mind that there will be no failure in life if you can learn and grow from your mistakes.

- **Protect yourself:** Try to bring the right people into your life. There will be friends who might just try to take pleasure in your pain instead of being happy with your success and happiness.

  You will have to identify such people and get rid of them as fast as possible. There is not enough time in life that you can actually waste on all those who desire to take away the shine on your face. As you do so, you will be able to respect and love yourself even more.

- **Live intentionally:** As you start to live your life with design and purpose, you will be able to love and accept yourself more, regardless of what takes place in your life. Try to understand that your purpose is not required to be absolutely clear. When you intend to live your life in a healthy and meaningful way, you can opt for decisions that will aid your intention.

  Also, you can start feeling good regarding yourself as you achieve success related to such a purpose. You can learn to love your own self to a greater extent as you see yourself attaining all that you prepare yourself to do. To do this, it is necessary to develop your intentions to live.

  If you decide to work on only one or some of the above-mentioned actions of self-love, you can easily start to love and accept yourself more. We will discuss all such actions in detail in the upcoming chapters. Try to think of the appreciation that you can give to yourself as you get to do any action of self-love. The more self-love anyone can have for themselves, the more prepared they can be for a hearty living. You can attract circumstances along with people in your direction that will aid your well-being.

Chapter 2: Self-Love and Its Obstacles

Let us be transparent and honest – at times, it is not as easy as we think it is to practice self-love. Regardless of your best intentions, it is tough to shake off old habits, belief systems, and mindsets that you have adopted and normalized for a long time. Like any goal you try to achieve, self-love has its own set of obstacles or barriers. But all that happens is that most often, we cannot determine and overcome the barriers. We fail to show ourselves true care along with affection that we all deserve.

So, while each of us might deal with our special set of obstacles when it is about self-love, certain barriers tend to be the most common on the journey. Luckily, as you get to identify them, you can start to recognize when they show up and how each of them might affect your life. It will help you to be intentional and proactive regarding deciding to be more self-loving.

You Keep Comparing

How many times have you found yourself scrolling down your social media and looking at a complete stranger or a close friend's latest photo or update? How many times have you felt a sense of insecurity, longing, or personal discontent from such things? Regardless of how strong all these feelings are as they crop up, they generally surface as comparisons.

Although it might seem like a normal tendency to see yourself in relation to other people, it is surely an unhealthy practice. It is especially the case when envy is in action. As you try to think adversely about all that you do or do not have or desire, all that is not yours, it will directly affect how you see yourself. It will make you experience a lack of confidence, appreciation of self, and contentment.

Trying to Be Overly Self-Critical

Being our biggest critic is definitely something that all of us struggle with. There are people who just continue to see themselves from this lens. It is because of all those things that we have experienced in childhood that fostered shame, guilt, low self-confidence, and unforgiveness for ourselves. In fact, some of us have already lived half of our lives being excessively self-critical.

But what we fail to understand is that it can be a huge barrier when it is about being self compassionate and self-loving. Such a challenge is even more apparent when someone finds it a lot easier to offer intangible gifts to other people while facing a tough time providing the same for themselves.

People Pleasing

All those who are kind-hearted or seek external validation or acceptance from other people are most likely to meet this obstacle at one point or the other. It does not indicate that being caring or kind regarding what other people think is an issue. However, when you turn out to be excessively concerned with the opinions of other people or feel worried that you might not get accepted, you might overextend yourself. You might give your all to try and find a sense of fulfillment from doing all those things that you think can make others happy. In the majority of cases, we end up doing so at the expense of our own well-being.

Zero Boundaries

Your energy, space, and time are required to be treated in a sacred way. Whenever there is an absence of self-love, you are most likely to find yourself lowering all your boundaries. Or you might not even have any boundaries after you place any negative value on yourself that tends to shape the way you see the importance of your own energy, space, and time. If this sounds common, you might find yourself giving zero attention to all such areas. You will provide others more access and privilege to such things if you fail to consider self-love in the equation.

No Attention to Your Needs

No matter if you believe it or not, your partner, best friend, siblings, boss, neighbors, and others are not mind readers. Loving yourself is all about being able to advocate for yourself in every relationship. Having the capability to determine and share your needs is necessary for all kinds of relationships. It also involves the kind of relationship that you hold with yourself. The moment you fail to pay attention to your needs and concentrate on others, you lose a part of yourself. Trying to fulfill the needs of others while putting your needs under the ground can act as a huge barrier to self-love. Self-love is mostly about taking care of the needs you have while paying attention to fulfilling them too.

No Time for Yourself

Spending quality time with others is a superb way to make them understand that you care for them. However, not having the same kind of time for yourself can be a huge challenge for you on your self-love journey. Carving out time for yourself is required to be held in high regard. If you cannot take out time for yourself or have no idea of the same, you can try out a technique. It is called "Stop, Drop, and Self-Care." In order to get started with this practice, you will need to set your alarm a few times every week and permit five to fifteen minutes so that you can do something good for yourself.

You might stay busy all day with your typical nine-to-five job. In that case, just move away from the work desk for a few minutes, and take a few deep breaths, walk, stretch, or meditate.

Just being able to acknowledge your physical presence can act as a healing technique. No matter what happens in life, having some time and spending it with yourself is of extreme importance.

Let Negativity Rule Over What Is Good

In our tiring everyday lives, one of the easiest things to do is to fixate on the frustrations. We try to dwell on an impossible goal, a bad day at work, or any situation that is not within our control. Having such a habit can stop you from moving ahead in life.

It acts like a major obstacle that might not be that easy to deal with. Allowing negativity to rule over good things can make self-love quite difficult. All you need to do in such moments is to concentrate on all that you have and feel grateful for the same. Negativity in any sector of life is a big "no."

Gloss Over Your Fears

Fear is a strong force. But it is not required to allow it to stop you from living the life that you dream of. Not being able to deal with your fears or glossing over your fears will not let you love yourself.

You will need to unpack the fear. The only way to deal with this obstacle is by making up your mind to go for it. Try to address all those things that frighten or trouble you. Just bring those up and talk about the same. Keep in mind that the more you can practice, the more you can move through your fears.

Exercise

Do you think there is anything that might stop you from loving yourself? It could be the case that the barriers in your life are more than one. Try to assess your life from the viewpoint of the above-mentioned obstacles and see if you find anything common with them in your life. If you do find any similarities, note them down.

Chapter 3: Emotional Awareness and Mindfulness

Emotional awareness or intelligence is the capability to tap into your emotions and utilize the same to make your life better. As you try to be in touch with your feelings, you will be able to manage your levels of stress besides communicating with others in a better way. These are the skills that are necessary to enhance your life personally and socially. Emotional awareness is necessary for self-love as it will let you tap into the emotions that you try to bury deep inside yourself. You can develop your emotional awareness with time.

How to Develop Emotional Awareness?

Here are some of the steps that you can follow to develop emotional awareness.

Note down emotional reactions to events during the day

It is quite easy to put all your feelings regarding what you experience during the day on the back burner. However, taking some time to acknowledge the way you feel about experiences is necessary to improve your emotional awareness. When you try to ignore your feelings, you will ignore essential information that tends to have a huge impact on your mindset. You will need to start to pay attention to your feelings besides connecting them to what you experience. For instance, suppose you are at work, and you get cut off in the middle of a meeting. What are the emotions that you feel at this moment?

On the other hand, what is your feeling as you get praised for great work? Being able to get into the practice of naming your emotions like embarrassment, sadness, contentment, or other feelings can help in enhancing your emotional awareness right away. Try to get into the habit of tapping into your emotional side at some points during the day.

Focus on your body

In place of trying to ignore the physical manifestations of your emotions, try to listen to them. Your body and mind are not separate. They can affect one another quite well. You can easily enhance your emotional intelligence by learning how you can read physical cues that makes you aware of the emotions you feel. For instance, stress might feel like having a tight chest, quick breathing, or a knot in the stomach. Or sadness might feel like getting up with heavy and slow limbs.

Observe how your behavior and emotions are linked

At times when you feel strong emotions, what is your reaction? You will have to tune into your gut responses to the situations you face daily in place of trying to react to them without any sort of reflection. The more you can get to know what tends to spur your behavioral impulses, the higher your emotional awareness will be. For instance, feeling insecure or embarrassed might make you withdraw from any conversation and disconnected. Feeling overwhelmed can make you panic and lose track of all that you are doing.

Do not judge your emotions

The emotions that you experience are all valid. In fact, your negative emotions are valid. But if you try to judge your emotions, you will inhibit your capability to feel them fully. You will end up making it tougher to use the emotions in a positive way. You can think of it in this way – every emotion you experience is a piece of new useful information linked to something in your world. Without access to such information, you will be left in the dark regarding how to react. It is the primary reason why the ability to feel your emotions is a kind of intelligence. It might be hard at first. However, you will have to practice allowing negative emotions to come up to the surface and linking them to what is happening. For instance, if you tend to feel envious, what is the emotion indicating about your situation?

Find patterns in your history of emotions

It is a great way to learn as much as possible regarding your feelings and the way they are connected to your life experiences. As you get a strong emotion, question yourself when was the last time you felt the same. What happened before and after? When you find out patterns, you get the power to exert more control over your behaviors. Try to observe the way you handled a particular situation in the past and how you will handle the same the next time.

Be agreeable and open-minded

Being agreeable and open actually go hand-in-hand when it is about emotional intelligence. Having a narrow mind is an indicator of lower emotional awareness. As you open your mind with internal reflection and understanding, it gets easier to take care of conflicts. You can find yourself being socially aware, and new kinds of possibilities will open up in front of you.

Improving empathy skills

Empathy is all about being able to recognize how others feel and sharing your emotions with them. Being a more active listener and focusing on what others are saying can help you better understand their feelings.

When you use the same information to inform decisions and improve relationships, that is a sign of emotional awareness. In order to improve empathy, you will have to start by putting yourself in the shoes of others. Try to think of how you would feel if you were present in the same situation.

As you see someone experiencing some sort of strong emotion, question yourself, "How would I react in this situation?" You will need to be interested in what is being said by other people so that you get the chance to react in a sensitive way.

Lower your stress by improving your emotional intelligence

Stress is the word that is used for feeling overwhelmed by various types of emotions. Our lives are packed with difficult situations. There are lots of stress triggers in such situations that can easily make any everyday issue seem more challenging than it actually is.

You will have to determine those things that tend to trigger your level of stress. Also, it is necessary to be aware of all those things that help in relieving the same. Try to get help if you require it.

Mindfulness and Self-Love

You must have heard of it before, but the most important connection that you have got in your life is with yourself. All of us have the tendency to love ourselves with conditions, rewarding ourselves when we do something we want. But we also judge ourselves harshly as we fall short of our expectations. The overall self-love journey is a challenge. Similar to any challenge, it needs patience, devotion, and practice. Mindfulness can be a great option if you are on your road to self-love. Being present fully while being able to listen to your inner voice can make you collected, calm, and a part of every moment. Here are some of the ways in which you can practice mindfulness for self-love.

Meditation

The most direct and fastest route to self-awareness while learning to truly love yourself is meditation. Meditation comes with the power to take you straight to your true self. It can teach you about compassion, forgiveness, along with acceptance. In simple terms, meditation helps in reconnecting us. It helps in awakening all those parts within yourself that are pure presence. As you get to meditate, you can get the true experience of deep inner calm and peace. You will learn to love yourself in the most authentic way, along with loving others.

Try out a body scan

One of the classic practices of mindfulness that can connect your body with your mind and let you find a haven within yourself is to try out a body scan. Close your eyes, zone in all your attention on every part of your body, right from the head to the toes. You can do this as slowly or quickly as you want. Do not try to judge each part or do not allow yourself to get distracted by discomfort or pain. All you need to do is focus on the way it feels. Is there any existence of tension? Are you gripping anywhere? You will have to allow yourself to find calm deep within the body and learn to appreciate it without any kind of judgment.

Get out in nature

Getting out into nature can be regarded as the easiest and quickest way to deal with negative energies and start feeling better. There is no need to find a mountain to climb. Going for a short walk after lunch to the park, heading out to see the sunset every evening, or a simple stroll in the garden can do the magic. Soon, you will find your mind wandering free, and you will crave to get close to nature.

Check the inner voice

The individual most of us talk to the most is ourselves. So, do you think you are being kind? A forgiving, empowering, and positive inner dialogue is necessary to support your self-love journey. Try to switch to something more positive as you sense negative thoughts creeping in. Concentrate on all that you can do differently the next time in place of thinking about what you did wrong. Try to start your day with positive affirmations and keep repeating them during the day as required.

Getting to know your personality type

Being able to understand your type of personality can help to have more compassion for yourself. In fact, you will be able to lift the veil from why you do the things you do. For instance, if you are an introvert and force yourself to get into the extrovert ideal, you might get frustrated with yourself. You get frustrated for feeling the internal introverted tendencies in place of trying to celebrate them. So, the more you can get to know who you are, the easier it will be for you to appreciate the things that make you different.

Stay positive with daily affirmations

The best way to ensure that your negative feelings no longer rob you of your joy is to repeat positive words to yourself on a daily basis. You can opt for mantras or affirmations that you can repeat throughout the day. It can help you to stay rooted in mindfulness. You can use affirmations like "slow down," "let it go," "stay focused," or "be here." As you feel overwhelmed by negative feelings or thoughts, try to repeat your mantra. Also, remember that you might not control everything that happens to you. However, you can always decide how to respond. Staying positive is the prime requirement of your self-journey, and also to be mindful. You can make a list of your daily affirmations and repeat the same as you need to.

Develop Emotional Awareness Using Mindfulness

Do you know that mindfulness can help in developing emotional awareness that can directly help you in self-love and developing better relationships with other people? Below are the tools that can help you get started.

Difficult conversations

When there is a presence of dissonance among people, disagreements are most likely to take place. In fact, leaders need to deal with tough conversations, and it is using this skill that conflict can be dealt with in relationships.

Mindfulness is the tool that can support you in building this capacity. It can help you, especially in developing the capability to understand the perspective of others so that you do not react from your point of view.

At times, in tough conversations, we tend to get stuck in our angle or perspective, which can easily trigger emotional reactions to the overall conflict. With the help of mindfulness practice, you can easily release yourself from the stuck place besides being able to understand your impact on other people. It can be done by taking a pause first and stopping yourself from reacting in a tough conversation with frustration or anger.

Mindfulness can help in keeping you more present in any conversation, along with the conversations with yourself. It ensures that you do not get overtaken by your wide array of emotions and connect back to the prefrontal cortex. The prefrontal cortex is the part of the brain that can help us in making rational decisions. Finally, with the help of mindfulness, you can easily understand and empathize with the other person's point of view. It can result in more win-win solutions taken from the perspectives of both people.

Compassion

It is the ability to move into action and be of service after you empathize with the emotions of another person. For instance, you might see that someone you know is emotionally triggered in the workplace. In place of trying to be reactive in such situations, try to ask how you can support them in the best way.

All of these, collectively, can help you build your emotional awareness that you can use for yourself and also for others. With all the benefits, don't you think mindfulness is worth giving a try?

Traits of Emotionally Intelligent People

Here are some common traits of emotionally intelligent people that you can learn from.

- **Utilizing assertive style of communication:** Communication of this kind can go a long way in the direction of earning respect without being too passive or aggressive. People who are emotionally aware know well how to communicate their needs and opinions directly while respecting others.

- **Responding in place of reacting to conflicts:** At times of conflict, feelings of anger along with emotional outbursts are quite common. Any person who is emotionally intelligent will know the ways in which they can be calm in times of tough situations. They stay away from making impulsive decisions that might otherwise result in larger problems. Also, they can understand that during any problem, the ultimate goal is to resolve the issue. Such people tend to concentrate on making sure that the words they say and their actions are aligned.

- **Being motivated:** Emotionally aware people tend to be self-motivated. The attitude they possess can motivate other people. They tend to be strong when faced with challenges.

- **Utilizing skills of active listening:** In meaningful communication, people who are emotionally aware listen to get clarity in place of waiting to speak up. Such people ensure that they properly grasp everything that is being communicated prior to their response. Also, they give close attention to all kinds of nonverbal details in any conversation.

  It helps in the prevention of misunderstandings, permits the speaker to respond in the right way, and also showcases respect for the individual they are communicating with.

- **Practicing ways for the maintenance of a positive attitude:** Never try to belittle the capability of your attitude. Having some sort of negative attitude can quickly infect other people when an individual permits it to. People who are emotionally aware come with great alertness for the moods of others who are with them and safeguard the attitude they possess according to that.

  Also, they know very well what is required to be done to have a great life while having an optimistic outlook. It could involve having a superb lunch or dinner, placing positive affirmations at their work desk, or opting for meditation or prayer during their day.

- **Taking critique well:** A necessary aspect of enhancing emotional awareness is being capable of taking critique. In place of trying to get defensive or offended, people with high emotional intelligence take some time to understand the source of the critique, how it affects others or their performance, and how they can resolve any issue in a constructive way.

- **Practicing self-awareness:** People who are aware emotionally are intuitive and self-aware. They know their emotions and the way they might affect the people surrounding them. Also, they grasp the emotions along with the body language of others and utilize that info to improve skills of communication.

- **Empathizing with other people:** People who are emotionally intelligent are aware of the ways in which they can empathize. They can accept very well that empathy is more like a feature that showcases emotional strength and has nothing to do with weakness. They can relate to other people on a basic level using empathy. It can open up doors for establishing understanding between people who come with varying opinions along with mutual respect.

- **Being sociable and approachable:** People who are emotionally aware are always approachable. They tend to smile besides showcasing a positive presence. Such people use correct social skills depending on the connection with the people they are with. Also, interpersonal skill is a common thing besides being well aware of how to initiate clear communication, no matter the communication is nonverbal or verbal. Many of the above-mentioned skills or traits might seem to be best suited for all those who can understand basic human psychology. Although high emotional intelligence skills can come easily to people who are empathetic naturally, anyone can develop them. You will only need to practice a bit more to be self-aware while being conscious of the way you interact with other people and also with yourself.

Exercise

If you are not sure which mindfulness exercise to opt for, you can opt for self-love mantras. It could be anything – phrases, words, or short sentences that can help you to concentrate on all those things that truly matter to you. As you come up with a mantra, follow these guidelines:

- The mantra could be anything from a word to various sentences; however, the shorter, the better.
- The mantra needs to remind you of anything that you have attained or something that you are good at.
- The mantra needs to make you feel good about yourself.

For instance, if you are proud of yourself for beating your addiction to smoking cigarettes, you can choose a mantra like, "I have overcome obstacles in the past, and I will keep overcoming obstacles."

Create and write your mantras here.

____

____

____

____

____

____

Chapter 4: Being Present

You have surely heard several times about the importance of being in the present moment. Also, you must have come across the same kind of advice, such as:

- Be present in your life.
- Do not get trapped in thinking of your future or the past – live in the now!
- All that you have got is this moment. Do not allow it to slip away.

All these things just come down to a simple message – it is important to be in the present moment. But it might not be that easy in the world we live in today. There will always be something coming up that you require to anticipate or prepare for. Provided the hectic schedules and fast pace that the majority of us maintain, the basic level of unhappiness, stress, and anxiety is the new standard. None of us might be able to understand it; however, such a habit to get trapped in the past and the future could easily wear you out. The only solution to this is what most individuals keep repeating – commitment and conscious awareness to stay in the "now."

Why Is Being Present So Important?

The concept of "here and now" or being in the present moment indicates that you are mindful and aware of all that is taking place at the current time. It involves not being disturbed by the ruminations of your past or tension of the future; however, centered on the moment. Being present-minded can be regarded as the key to staying happy and healthy. It can help you deal with anxiety, reduce rumination and worrying, and will keep you connected and grounded to every possible thing around you and yourself. In fact, it could help you cope with pain in an effective way and reduce stress.

Why Is It Tough to Stay In the Present Moment?

Being able to live in the present moment tends to be hard as most of us are always taught to worry about the future or just ruminate on the past. Reminders, advertisements, messages, alerts, and notifications are always directed in the direction of the future or the past. Try to recall how often you get busy doing anything important when you get out of the flow by the sound of the phone. Now, try to give this a thought - how often do your notifications or messages help you to be aware of the current moment. In case you are like me, the response from your side will be, "Just never." The smartphone is a great piece of technology that lets you do so much more. But it is necessary to take a break from your phone at regular intervals. Some of the primary factors that might also dedicate to the incapability of living in the present are:

- All of us experience a great deal of uncertainty while being in the present moment, which might lead to anxiety.

- Our minds wander around.
- We try to edit the bad parts of any experience.

It might be hard to fight all such factors; however, none of us are slaves to mind tendencies. It is always achievable to make better choices in life and overcome all kinds of harmful or destructive urges.

Balance Your Past, Present, Future

At times, it is okay to have some thoughts regarding your future and past. Where would you find yourself if you failed to have a look at your past achievements and mistakes and get valuable learning from the same? What would be your position in life if you failed to plan the future or prepare yourself for all that is about to happen? You are most likely not to be in a great place in both instances. But all that is needed to live a great life is to balance all kinds of thoughts of your present, future, and past. Trying to think of any of these excessively can lead to negative effects on your life. However, keeping them in balance is all that can help you to be happy. It is tough to indicate what the right balance is. But you can be aware of when you have hit it as you will worry less, experience less stress, and find yourself spending most of your time in the present.

Guidelines to hit the balance

To maintain a healthy balance, you will have to keep certain guidelines in mind.

- Try to think of your past in limited doses besides ensuring that you concentrate on the past for some sense.

- Think of your future in limited doses while you ensure that you concentrate on the same in a healthy and low-anxiety way.

- Be in the current situation most of the time.

  Indeed, abiding by the above-mentioned guidelines is easier said than being done. However, it will turn out to be easier for you with practice.

Be in the moment and make plans for your future

The whole thing might seem a bit complex as you determine such a sensitive balance; however, it is not as complicated as it feels. As you opt for mindfulness, you are not denying or ignoring any future or past thoughts. You only choose not to reside on the same. It is absolutely natural to label and acknowledge your future- and past-focused things while being aware of their overall importance. But what is more important here is to not permit yourself to get swayed away by thinking about the future or past. As you are aware and present, you are not required to worry about getting captivated by your past thoughts or anxiety regarding your future. You can always revisit your past and just anticipate all that is to come without losing yourself. Awareness of the present moment can be regarded as a superb way to reduce your worries. Here are some tips to be attuned to your present besides getting rid of excessive anxiety.

- Practicing relishing can help. Just stop worrying about your future by allowing yourself to experience the present fully.

- Find the flow and make the best use of your time by having no track of the same.

- Concentrate on breathing. Let mindfulness smoothen your interactions with other people and make you peaceful.

- Enhance engagement by cutting down your mindlessness moments while paying attention to new stuff so that you can enhance mindfulness.

- Improve your ability to accept by moving in the direction of what is bothering you instead of trying to run away from it.

The power of yoga

You will surely not get surprised by hearing that yoga can be a great way to build a connection with the present besides being in the moment. You will come across plenty of reasons why yoga can turn out to be supportive of mindfulness. However, a primary reason is a concentration on your breath. The prime roadway to presence can be achieved via your body-mind connection. The breath is always the here and now, and it can be regarded as the ultimate present moment. It is said that your breath is the continuous connection with the here and now. The overall presence of your life is fixed in the flow. As you concentrate all your focus on your breathing, you will get no other option than to be in the present moment.

In order to get your attention back to the current situation at times of stress, there is a breathing exercise that you can try. You can do the same when you feel overwhelmed about your future or past. When you inhale, say to your own self, “I am breathing in.” As you exhale, say, “I am breathing out.” On your next cycle of breath, say, “I am here, and this is now.” Such an easy exercise can help in bringing you back to the moment without any delay. In fact, it comes with the power to drag a rigid mind that is full of stress or worries. One more aspect that is linked to yoga that permits you to increase your awareness of the present is the poses or postures that you make. You will see that the moment you opt for a nice pose, the mind will get filled up with restless thoughts. No matter how irritating this might feel, it can be considered a great thing.

It is an indication that you are starting to process all your stress while pushing yourself to the point where mindfulness can be practiced. The smooth flow from one starting position to another one can be regarded as a chance to cultivate your capacity to be present.

Simple Exercises for Strengthening Awareness of Current Moment

In case the above-mentioned breathing exercise seems useful, you can opt for a bunch of other exercises that will help you boost mindfulness along with the sense of the present moment. Let's have a look at some of them.

Doing a body scan mindfully

The act is a superb option to push ourselves into a mindful mood besides being in touch with our bodies. Being able to do this early morning every day could help in starting the day with a relaxed mind. As you lie down or sit on your bed, try to take a few mindful and deep breaths. Try to notice the air gets in and out of the lungs. Beginning from the toes, concentrate all the attention on a single area of the body. Be attentive to the way the body part feels. You will also have to determine sensations if you experience anything. After you are done with some time of concentrated attention, you can opt for the next body area or part.

It is not only an effective way of putting ourselves in a mindful state, but it can also make us understand when our bodies feel different from normal. In fact, you might catch an illness or injury that you might not notice normally. With the help of this exercise, you can easily get to know so.

Writing in a journal

A great exercise to help fix the perfect tone of mindfulness for your day is to start journaling. It can be more effective when done right after you wake up. Right after you wake up in the morning, prior to heading off to your work/checking things on the to-do list, take some time to make an entry in your journal. You can opt for one new page daily. You can also just write down the thoughts that come to your mind at that moment.

Visualizing daily goals

Being able to visualize your goals can be a great way to be mindful on a daily basis besides being able to follow through with your goals. As you set your daily goals, take some time to visualize each of them. Visualize yourself undertaking each of your goals and getting done with them. It will help you more if you can get as much detail as possible in your visualization. You need to try to make it feel real and also within reach.

When you find yourself ticking off an everyday goal from the list, start with the next goal. Keep repeating the process until you are done with visualizing all your goals. Trying to visualize your goal completion will not only aid in enhancing concentration but can also lower your levels of stress. It can help in the improvement of your performance and provide you with the motivation or energy that you will need to attain the goals on the list.

Taking a mindful walk in nature

Try to take support from the beauty of nature that exists around you. It could be a superb option to practice mindfulness. When you get the urge to go for a walk, no matter if it is a short stroll in your neighborhood or a long walk in a scenic spot, try to turn it into a mindful nature walk. It is the easiest thing to make any kind of walk mindful. You will only need to guide all the senses in staying aware of all that is going on within you and around you.

Exercise

In case you are a late riser, try to start your day early in the morning, followed by gratitude. As you start your day with gratitude, you can train the mind to look for positive things instead of concentrating on frustrations and challenges. The key to making this exercise effective is not the time you spend in gratitude or the number of things you feel grateful for. It is about the focused intensity and the feelings you have around your effort. Try to do this for a few days and note down the differences in your daily life.

What am I greatful for ?

Differences that gratitude made in my life?

Chapter 5: Accepting Yourself the Way You Are

Self-acceptance is the capability of a person to value all parts of themselves without any kind of condition. It indicates that you value all your good parts and the parts required to be improved. The overall process of self-acceptance starts right from acknowledging judgments against your own self and then softening the judgments so that you can value all your parts. Also, it is necessary to commit yourself to altering your focus from blame and judgment to compassion and tolerance.

Acknowledging Your Attributes and Strengths

Acknowledging the attributes you value or your strengths is necessary to balance all the work you will do for accepting your undervalued parts. In fact, being able to realize your strengths can also help to alter your conceptualization of yourself. You can start by making a list of all your strengths or by listing one strength every day if it feels challenging for you to think of them. For instance:

- I am a talented painter.
- I am a strong parent.
- I am a kind person.
- I am great at solving problems.

Making a List of Accomplishments

Try to identify and acknowledge your strengths by enlisting all your accomplishments. It can include the people you have helped, the troublesome times you have dealt with, or your personal achievements. Such things can help you to focus on deeds or actions. Here are some other examples that can help you to identify your strengths in a better way.

- I made it a goal to run a marathon, and after two months of proper training, I touched the finish line.

- The death of my father was quite hard on my entire family. However, I am proud of myself as I was able to support my mother to deal with all the hardships.

- After I lost my job, it was tough to adjust and pay my bills. But I learned some great things about my strength, and I am in a better position now.

Recognizing the Way You Judge Yourself

Being able to recognize your judgment is necessary to help you identify the areas where you tend to be overly critical of yourself. Being excessively critical of yourself is when you develop areas or determine attributes of yourself that you have got unproductive feelings about. It might involve disappointment or shame, and such feelings are powerful enough to squash self-acceptance. You will have to start by preparing a list of negative thoughts that you tend to have about yourself.

- I am too fat.
- I can never do anything right.
- I always take the comments of other people the wrong way.
- I am bad at making decisions.

Finding Out How Comments of Other People Affect You

As others comment about us, we tend to internalize such comments and keep working them into all our opinions about ourselves. As you get to determine the root of all kinds of self-judgments, you will be able to rethink the way you perceive yourself. For instance, if your friends criticize your looks all the time, you might not be that confident regarding your looks at present. However, you will have to understand that their criticisms were rooted in their own insecurities. As you get to realize this, you will be able to rethink your overall confidence regarding your looks. The same thing can be applied to the other areas of life too.

Catching Yourself As You Have Negative Thoughts

As you are aware of the particular areas of your life for which you tend to be the most critical, it is now time to quiet the inner critic. The inner critic that we all have got tends to tell us, "I can never do anything right" or "I am fat." As you successfully quiet the inner critic, you will be able to reduce reinforcement of all kinds of negative thoughts regarding yourself. You will be able to create room for forgiveness, acceptance, and compassion. In order to quiet the inner critic, you will have to catch the negative thoughts the moment they come up. For instance, if you find yourself thinking, "I am an idiot," you can ask yourself:

- Does the thought make me feel good?
- Can it be regarded as a kind thought?
- Would I ever say this to a loved one or friend?

If all your answers are "no," you will be able to know that your inner critic is speaking.

Challenging the Inner Critic

The moment you find yourself having negative thoughts about yourself, you will need to challenge and quiet your inner critic. You will need to be prepared with a positive mantra or counter-thought.

You can also use all the strengths that you have determined in the previous steps. For instance, if you find yourself saying, "I am not intelligent," try to change the thought to a kind statement.

You can say, "Although I might not know this topic, I am intelligent in other areas. It is completely okay." You will have to keep reminding yourself of all your strengths. Also, try to remind the inner critic that negative statements are not true at all. Keep reminding and teaching yourself as you are still learning to change your thoughts about yourself.

Concentrate on Self-Acceptance Before Self-Improvement

Self-acceptance is all about accepting yourself the way you are in the current moment. Self-improvement is about the changes that are required to be made to accept yourself in the future. You will have to determine the areas with the intention of valuing them as they are in the moment. Then, you can make up your mind whether you would like to improve them in the future or not.

For instance, you might want to lose weight. You will need to start with self-acceptance first. Say, "Even though I want to lose weight, I feel good the way I am." Now, try to frame self-improvement in productive and positive terms. In place of trying to think, "I do not have the ideal body shape, and as I lose ten pounds, I can be beautiful," say, "I would love to lose ten pounds so that I have more energy and feel healthier."

Change Expectations of Yourself

As you set unrealistic expectations for yourself, you are most likely to set yourself up for disappointment. It will tend to make it tough to accept yourself. So, you will need to shift your expectations of yourself.

For instance, if you say, "I am so lazy, and I haven't even cleaned the bed today," you will have to alter your expectations and say, "I made dinner for my family. I can clean the bed tomorrow."

Learning That You Are Worthy of Compassion

It might seem uncomfortable or odd to say that you will develop compassion for yourself as it might seem to be self-centered. However, most of us fail to understand that self-compassion is the bedrock of self-acceptance. It is because compassion can be regarded as the sympathetic consciousness of the distress of others with the desire to alleviate the same.

You also deserve the same kind of kindness and understanding. The very first step that comes in self-compassion is to validate your self-worth. It is common and easy to allow the thoughts, opinions, beliefs, and feelings of other people to dictate your self-approval. In place of letting your approval be other's decision, try to make it your own. You will have to learn to approve and validate yourself without any need for it from other people.

Practicing Forgiveness

When you start practicing self-forgiveness, it can help in the reduction of your guilt feelings from the past, which might stop you from accepting the present "you" fully. Most of us tend to judge our past based on unrealistic expectations. As you forgive yourself, it can help in lifting your shame besides providing you more room to develop a new and accepting view of the past. At times, the inner critic is reluctant enough to allow you to forgive yourself for the past. Sometimes we tend to be unkind to ourselves simply by carrying guilt around. Try to take note of the guilt that you might have. You will need to evaluate if there exists any kind of external factors that are involved in the overall situation. Events might not be within your control all the time, but still, you hold on to the feelings of guilt. Try to evaluate whether the actions were truly out of control.

In order to practice self-forgiveness, the exercise of writing a letter to yourself can be a powerful tool to initiate the process. Try to write a letter addressing your past or younger self. Make sure that you use a loving and kind tone. The aim is to remind your younger self that you might have made mistakes. But you are aware that you are not perfect, and that is completely okay. Try to keep in mind that the mistakes you make can provide you with valuable learning opportunities.

Exercise

Listing your accomplishments should not be a tough thing. It can help you to be proud of yourself even more. But a great exercise would be to note down daily achievements as you get back home from work or right before going to bed. Try to think of your day or the things that happened during the course of the day. Now, note down all those things that you think could be achievements for you. It is not needed to be anything huge. Simple things like reaching the office on time or getting done with your house chores without any frustration would count. You will have to try and include at least one achievement every day. You can have a full list of accomplishments by the end of the month.

Chapter 6: Getting Rid of the Past

Troubling memories from your past can make it tough for you to be in the present. In case you face some tough time moving on from things that took place in your life, you might start to heal with the help of acknowledging the way in which the past has given shape to the individual you are in the present day. We will discuss some easy steps in this section that will help you get rid of the past and enjoy your present life.

Acknowledging Past Challenges

Unresolved experiences from the past can easily lead to everlasting physiological along with psychological effects. In such instances, it is necessary to get acquainted with the way in which your past might be affecting your present habits or outlook. The first step is to stop yourself from pretending that the past does not affect you. You can never move away from your past without accepting it.

In case anything takes place that triggers strong reactions or keeps reminding you of traumatic events, you will need to acknowledge that it is the situation. Allow your own self to feel all that you feel regarding your past. For instance, when you go to any social situation that tends to trigger strong emotions about your past, try not to avoid them. Excuse yourself for some time and step away. Then, try to reflect on the past for some moment and how it tends to affect you right before you rejoin the group.

Accepting You Can Never Change All That Happened

You could never visit your past. However, it is possible to change how you perceive it and handle the same. Your hurt version will keep carrying over the emotional pain into new relationships and experiences if you fail to do so. The efforts from your side are required to be directed in the direction of accepting past events and forgiving all those who you think have been wrong to you.

Feel the emotions that you possess regarding the past. After that, allow all such feelings to go. As you feel sorrow or anger regarding your past, you will need to check in with yourself that being with such negative emotions will harm you in the long term. Anger or any of its forms can never undo all that took place in the past. Try to acknowledge all that you feel. The process is time-consuming and is going to vary for every individual.

Spending Time With Others

Unresolved experiences from the past can make it feel impossible to trust new individuals in life. It can make it difficult for you to develop healthy relationships. But having strong social support can act as the best force in healing the overall effects of damaging experiences. It is necessary to feel supported around people in contrast to feeling frightened. So, try to take things slowly, like just meeting a new individual for coffee. Another great way to be comfortable interacting with others again is volunteering. It can help in being more comfortable with all kinds of vulnerabilities when you get a view of other people bearing their own.

Evaluating Your Social Circle

You can consider leaving behind friends who tend to make you focus on your past. Your social environment that you are a part of can define who you are. In fact, it can affect the way in which you incorporate unresolved past experiences into your life. Try to spend more time thinking of all those individuals you have been with and how such people tend to make you feel.

In case you feel that there exist individuals whose aim is to reinforce negative habits or make you feel bad, you can think of spending as little time as possible with such people.

For instance, friends who try to belittle you all the time might not be the right thing to allow in your life. You can think of making new friends or opt for a change in scenery. It might not be as easy as it sounds. However, it can be regarded as a superb way of making you cross the boundary of your comfort zone and develop as an individual.

It is also great to opt for new hobbies with other or new peers. As you feel you are prepared, try pushing the comfort zone boundaries by being part of a local art class or basketball team, or any other sports team. As you do so, new life directions will slowly emerge that might not have been possible otherwise.

Being Grateful for Companions Who Provide You Support

Do not get sad while you think about all those individuals who failed to appreciate or respect you. In place of that, focus on those people who stood by your side all the time. You will have to make them aware that you appreciate their support and help. It can be a tough thing to prevent yourself from dwelling on negativity. However, your true companions are the ones who need all the attention.

You will have to keep good friends close to you during this time. It will let you feel confident enough so that you can engage with difficult emotions or past experiences without feeling lonely. As you get the feeling that you might be slipping, try to spend your time around a person you trust and who can help you to be on track.

Engaging With Your Fears Followed by Changing Your Habits

At times, most of us tend to build habits that make us distant from confrontation or to move beyond unresolved experiences. You will need to develop habits that can help deal with bad habits. For instance, you might be scared of dogs.

Or, if a dog ever attacked you, you might develop the habit of crossing the street as you see someone coming with a dog. In fact, you might get to a point with this that you do it without even thinking of it. It can help in reducing your anxiety in the short term. However, it might stop you from dealing with all your fears in the long run.

In such an instance, you could try from your side to make some effort so that you can break the habit. There is no need to seek out dogs; however, you can stop the behavior of crossing any street as you find a dog coming.

As you turn out to be comfortable with it, you can also ask an unknown person if you can pet his/her dog. With time, it can help you get rid of the trauma.

Also, you might not be able to have a look at the way in which unresolved experiences changed you. Your tries to stay away from them get ingrained in your everyday habits. A great option to be aware of behavioral changes is to question a person who is close to you whether they sense anything odd in your behavior.

For instance, after breaking up with your partner, you can question a friend, “Have I been acting in a weird way since I broke up with him/her?”

Exercise

Think of past challenges or unhappy moments and make a list of them. The next thing that you will need to do is to look at each of them and find out if you get any thoughts in your mind regarding those moments. If you get any thought, pick that up and give your best to use it in a positive way. For instance, if you feel bad for not being able to get your dream job in the past, use that feeling in a positive way in the present. Try to use the same as your new motivation and set one thing in mind – "I will have to show myself that I can get that job and I am capable of it."

Chapter 7: Stop Blaming Yourself

Too often in life, you might find yourself apologizing for things or situations that might be out of your control. But what is the reason behind this? It is because most of us tend to feel that we need to be at fault for anything going wrong as we are in charge of our own lives. We all make mistakes. It is a cliché that you might or might not believe. But it is true.

You might come across the success story of a person and think, "He has to succeed as he does everything right." But it is not correct. The prime difference between successful and unsuccessful people is that successful people stop blaming themselves for any mistake. They can easily move past their mistakes so that they can move ahead in life. Trying to dwell on a bad decision will only exacerbate the negative feelings you have got for yourself. It might seem tough, but you will have to stop blaming yourself for reaching where you want to be. You will need to learn how you can forgive yourself.

Things You Should Not Blame Yourself For

Here are certain things that you should stay away from blaming yourself for.

Your emotions

What if you cry excessively, get too concerned, or get excessively passionate about anything that matters to you? You will need to understand that there is no existence of "too much" when it is about your feelings. The sooner you can learn this, the better will be your emotional health.

How do you handle those emotions

Try to write down everything that you think of in a letter. Try slamming a door and do not even feel guilty about it. Opt for a walk and turn off your phone. You can do anything that you require to process all that you are going through. Anything you do, you will have to do it unapologetically. All of us handle our challenges in our own designed way. So, there is no need to blame yourself for how you handle your emotions.

Rejection of someone else

It is never your fault that some other person does not like your hair, the way you carry yourself, or your stance on politics. That is completely their own problem. When you behave in a way that you feel is most authentic to you, that is everything that you can do. The correct people, the ones who think of you, will be able to accept every inch of it.

Small failures

No matter small or big, failures can be regarded as a natural part of human life. All of us are humans, and it can be said that mistakes are in our nature. You try to forgive other people for their indiscretions. It is high time now that you start to extend yourself the same kind of courtesy.

Your requirements

Every human being is incredibly complicated. So, it can be said that our requirements or necessities will also be different. There is no need to blame yourself for requiring certain components from a career or a relationship that might not be that necessary to someone else. Never apologize for knowing all that it takes to make you feel fulfilled.

Being bad at something

Some people are born with the capability of crafting incredible things from a coffee table, whereas others end up burning themselves while using a hot glue gun. You will have to understand that life is a series of trials and errors. You have got your own set of unique gifts that you can offer the world and that are also different from someone else's.

Your guilty pleasures

If you love watching animated movies with a large pizza, there is nothing to be ashamed of. In fact, it is also acceptable to enjoy your time during happy hours, meditating every night, or dating around. You love all that you love. So, try embracing it and stay away from hiding it.

Putting yourself before some other person

The connection and relationship you have with your mind, soul, and heart can be regarded as the most important relationship anyone can have. So, there is nothing wrong with being a bit selfish when the time actually calls for it.

Terminated relationship

Some individuals are not just meant to be a part of our lives beyond the lessons that they teach us. It is nothing more complex than this. The ones who have to stay will stay. There is no need to blame yourself when you cannot hold someone in your life.

Trusting a person you should not have

Feeling betrayed or burned by a person can swallow you as a whole. However, the actions are their own, and it has got nothing to do with you. Human beings are flawed. At times, such flaws might get showed up in the starting; sometimes, they might not reveal themselves until a few years have passed.

If you keep your walls up every time you meet new people to protect yourself from getting hurt, you will end up living a life of sheer loneliness. Nothing can be worse than that.

Things that happened in the past

Dwelling in the past is more or less like getting up every day and putting on some hideous fashion trend that dates back to the earlier decade. We all come with the power to make the choice of living in the "now."

Any sort of event, negative or otherwise, only belongs to the time period when it took place. The only direction that we all can move in is forward. There is nothing more beautiful than that.

Stop Blaming Yourself and Move Ahead in Life

The life that all of us have got is quite short. So, why waste it by blaming ourselves and getting stagnated in one place? There could be nothing more refreshing and motivating than being able to forgive yourself. Here are some of the ways in which you can stop blaming yourself and enjoy the course of life.

Take responsibility without placing blame

As you get to take responsibility for your actions, you can easily accept that you made some mistakes. Never try to shift the blame on someone else. It requires a strong-willed person to confidently admit that they have made a mistake. It is required to be done so that you can clear your conscious. When you fail to accept responsibility for your actions, you will risk having other people blame you throughout your life relentlessly. Simply by accepting responsibility, you get to clear that you were wrong, and now all you want is to work on bettering yourself.

Loving yourself

As you blame yourself, you end up casting your own self in a negative light. But the moment you take responsibility for all your actions, you can concentrate on the positive traits. All you need to do is to be kind to yourself besides being realistic about your shortcomings. You will need to be aware of your strengths too. As you do so, you will be able to focus on strengthening your weaknesses and supplementing the positive aspects related to your personality.

Seeking out help

There exists a huge misconception that seeking mental help indicates a sign of weakness. It is not at all true. In fact, as you decide to see a therapist, it is an indication that you desire to get better. Never allow the social stigma of getting in touch with a therapist or mental health professional to dissuade you from seeking the help you require. Never think twice before seeking help. It is especially the case when you get to indulge in self-blame every now and then.

Helping others

There is no doubt that all of us have got many talents. However, as you tend to spend all your days in self-pity, you can never get to use them. Try to use your expertise to help others and give back to the community you are a part of. As you do so, you can feel yourself floating farther away from all the mistakes that you might have made in the past. You will need to start defining yourself by all kinds of charitable actions that you opt for. In fact, volunteering can be regarded as a superb way to get some perspective on the world that exists around you. Also, it could turn out to be a way of finding the true calling of life.

Forgiving freely

As said earlier – everyone makes mistakes. The very first step in forgiving yourself for any mistake is to try to be more forgiving to other people. As you get to properly understand that everyone in this world makes mistakes, you will be able to forgive yourself more easily. There is no need to be perfect as no one else is or could be. All you need to do is be the best that you can ever be. It all starts with forgiving yourself and being able to move on with your life.

Stop being critical

If you tend to be critical of yourself, the chances are high that you will be critical of other people too. You might do so even without realizing the same. Trying to judge others could be nothing more than wasting your time, the time you could have used to better yourself in some way or the other. You will have to try and see things from the point of view of other people. In fact, all those people who have been judging other people tend to be paranoid and keep thinking that others are judging them. As you successfully let go of the idea that others are out to get you, you can get free to live your life in the best way.

Learning and moving on

A mistake that gets repeated more than one time cannot be regarded as a mistake. If you failed to learn the first time, you should not expect others to sympathize with you the second time you mess up. You will have to own up to the actions you make and use your experiences in the form of stepping stones.

Never allow yourself to be stagnant. Also, you will need to stop yourself from falling into old patterns or habits. If nobody made mistakes in their lives, nobody would have been able to improve themselves. Try to keep moving forward and carry the knowledge that you got from the toughest situations.

Why Is Change a Good Thing?

It is rightly said that nothing is permanent in life except change. Change is inevitable. The most prominent kind of change that we tend to experience every day is time itself. We meet new people, move to different places, and lose our loved ones along the way during our lifetime. As change cannot be avoided, it might be better for you if you can learn to embrace it. When you do that, you will get to realize that change can bring about lots of new experiences and opportunities in life that are good for you.

If everything in life remained the same, your life would have become dull besides being monotonous. It is in human nature to get bored of something quite quickly and demand new things. It is often required to change your mind and deal with things in different manners.

If you fail to be flexible enough to alter your mind, you will not be able to move on and attain your life goals. So, it is necessary that you start thinking of changes in a more positive way and also be ready for them. There are people who tend to fear change as they feel there might be some negative effect on their life and career. However, as you get to realize that resisting or fighting change is tougher than accepting it, you will find that it is for your good to be with changing circumstances. You might alter the setting of your bedroom or wardrobe to feel good. Also, it can help in getting rid of depression and stress.

You can regard change as fuel for your life. When there is no change at all, your life is most likely to come to a standstill. You can think of change as a dear friend who can console you in tough times.

You can experience new things

When you fail to work actively on evolving yourself, life will turn out to be stagnant. Learning new skills, being open to change, or working on yourself can help bring about changes that you were not even aware of are possible. It can help in unlocking all those opportunities that you have no idea about.

Improves life quality

For instance, taking a leap of faith and leaving a corporate job to get started with your business might seem like a huge risk. But you can also enjoy the benefits that you haven't experienced before. In this case, you can get the freedom to work when you want besides having more time to spend with your family.

Replaces worn-out and old things

You might have a favorite pair of jeans that you love the most. However, it does not fit you well or has got old. It is time to replace the same with well-fitted new pair of jeans. Such simple action of replacing an old thing with a new one can breathe new life into your home and your closet. Change is the only thing that can rescue you from old and worn-out things so that you can enjoy things in life.

It brings excitement and adventure to life

It is one of the easiest things to get sucked into your daily grind of going to work, getting back home, completing chores, scrolling your social media, and cruising through every day without any kind of excitement. In order to keep things interesting in life, try to plan activities that you can enjoy.

For instance, you can take classes on a skill that you want to learn, ask your friends to do something new together, or prepare a list of things that you can try out. As you successfully open up yourself to new experiences, it can easily invite excitement in your life.

You can think outside the box

There is nothing else that can feel as good as a new start. When you shake up your everyday routine with radical change, you will be able to open yourself to new opportunities that you might have ignored your whole life. Try to switch things on weekdays.

You can also plan to go for a walk every day but take a different route each time. Opting for small changes of this sort can help you in developing bigger changes.

You can be more grateful

At times, change chooses you, and it can take you out of your comfort zone without asking you for it. As you let go of your old habits, behaviors, or comforts, it can be hard for you.

But you will also be able to get a new perspective on life. When you embrace change, you can feel grateful that you possess the resilience and strength to do so.

It teaches you to live with your wounds

Experiencing a breakup or losing someone close to you, for instance, can result in lots of distress. You might think that time can be the only healer.

But there are various changes that you can introduce in your life so that you can speed up the process. Deciding to concentrate on those things or people that are still there in your life, taking up new activities or hobbies can help in occupying that time as you heal.

Exercise

Change might not feel that easy. But if you think that your life is getting stagnated or if you feel bored in your everyday routine or life, it is time to invite change. Try to make a list of all those things that you think have been with you for a long time. Ask yourself, "Are they needed any longer?" "Can I replace them with new things? or "Is change the only thing that can help me deal with life problems?" Try to answer these questions for every item or thing on your list. After you are done with your answers, figure out new things to change the old ones.

Chapter 8: How Can You Forgive Others?

Being able to forgive other people is a process that requires effort and time. If you were cheated by a partner, abused by a parent, or attacked by some unknown person, forgiving the individual who hurt you might seem unnecessary and impossible. It is truer when the person who hurt you does not accept what they did or cannot feel sorry for their action.

But you will need to understand that forgiveness is not at all something that you will do for other people. It is something that you will need to do for yourself. Forgiveness needs proper processing of what occurred and the way it impacted you. It also involves finding out ways to let go of the pain, desire for revenge, and anger. As you get to make peace with all that happened, you will be able to let it go and just move ahead in life.

Why Is Forgiveness Necessary?

Trying to hold on to the anger and pain caused by anyone who harmed you in any way is not at all good for you. All those who decide not to forgive might experience issues with their mental and physical health. It might include a weakened immune system, cardiovascular issues, along with enhanced depression and anxiety.

As you try to concentrate on the hurt in place of healing, you might keep repeating the negative experience. Such kind of negative thought loop might perpetuate the anger, pain, and other tough emotions that you experience at the time of the first offense. But as you forgive, you can easily release all kinds of negative emotions along with the energy that you were focusing on. Also, as you forgive those people who are close to you, it is possible to reestablish trust.

Expressing Yourself

While contemplating how to forgive someone, you might think that you will have to discuss the issue before you can try to forgive. It might help in expressing yourself or your feelings to the other person; however, it also might not. When the relationship is necessary or important for you and you want to maintain the same, you might find it helpful to tell the other person.

You will have to do so in non-threatening language and explain how their actions actually affected you. When the person has no existence in your life, if you wish to end the relationship, or if you think that the situation will get worse if you try to address it, you can just write a letter, tear it, and move on. Being able to write it down, even when you have no plans of sharing it, can help in forgiving someone. People are not required to be aware that you have forgiven them. The act of forgiveness is more for yourself compared to the other person.

Looking for the Positive

Journaling about the situation where you were wronged or hurt can help you process all that happened and move ahead in life. But how you write about the same and what you select to concentrate on can make a huge difference in how simple or easy it gets to forgive a person.

It can be quite helpful if you can journal about the benefits that you have received from any negative situation instead of the emotions you experience surrounding the event. Such strategies can help you forgive and move on easily. So, take a pen and try to journal about the silver lining the next time you come across someone raining on your parade. Or you can also maintain a gratitude journal so that you get to practice forgiveness every day.

Cultivating Empathy

There is no need to agree with what someone else did to you. But as you work on forgiving someone, it can help if you can put yourself in the shoes of the other person. It is said that empathy, especially with men, is linked to forgiveness. It can help in making the whole process a lot easier. In place of seeing them as your enemy, you will have to try and understand the factors that he/she was dealing with. Have you ever made the same kind of mistake? Were they experiencing a hard time in their lives? You will have to try and remember the good qualities of the other person. Also, try to assume that their overall motives were not to cause you any pain purposely. Such an approach might help you to find it easier to forgive.

Protecting Yourself and Moving On

You must have heard of the saying, "First time, shame on the other person; second time, shame on me." At times, it is tough to forgive when you feel that forgiveness can leave you open to the same kind of negative treatments in the future. It is necessary to understand that forgiveness is not at all similar to accepting the offending action. So, it is okay for you to include plans of self-protection for the future as a small part of the process of forgiveness. For instance, if you have a coworker who tends to steal all your ideas continuously, gossip about you, or belittle you in front of others, such negative behavior might be hard for you to forgive.

There are certain things that you can do to free yourself from the negative situation, like not sharing your ideas anymore. You will not need to hold a grudge for your protection.

Getting Help if You Require

Sometimes, it can be tough to forget the past and opt for forgiveness. It is especially true when the offending acts were traumatic. If you still face hardships regarding how you can forgive someone who wronged you, you might have better chances of success if you can work with a therapist.

A therapist can provide you with all the help so that you can work through your feelings internally and the therapist will support you personally throughout the process. A review from 2018 found that an approach called forgiveness therapy can help in the improvement of various aspects of well-being and psychological functioning. Forgiveness can help reduce anger, relieve depression, lower stress, and also improves positive emotions.

As you get hurt, being able to figure out how you can forgive someone can turn out to be a hard task. The above-mentioned strategies can surely help you to let go of your past stress and move on in your life. Remember that forgiving someone is an act that you are doing for yourself. When you successfully let go of your past, you can move ahead with a new and helpful perspective.

Exercise

If you think you have been wronged by someone in the past and you cannot forgive them, take a pen and try to write down the good qualities of the related person or the qualities that you love about them. Do not judge all that you write. As you do so, you will find that their good qualities outnumber the bad acts that they did to you. Indeed, you can never forget what they did, but this exercise can make forgiving them easier for you.

Chapter 9: Developing a Growth Mindset and Visualizing Your Future

What if your learning potential was something that you were never aware of? What if you are not aware of all that you could attain in the next few years? It is quite common for most of us where we do not even know where our work or effort can actually take us. The amount that any person can achieve always comes down to one thing – their mindset.

To be more particular, it is a growth mindset. A growth mindset is an idea that, with a bit of effort, it is always possible to enhance levels of intelligence, abilities, and talents. In order to understand the growth mindset in the best way, it is necessary to learn about another mindset. It is the fixed mindset. A fixed mindset is more like a belief that your talents and intelligence are static.

What Is the Point of Having a Growth Mindset?

Apart from everything else, a growth mindset is necessary for learning. When you can believe that your skills and talents are not static and that you can grow and adapt, you will be able to dedicate more effort to every life aspect. When you cultivate a growth mindset, you:

- Start to find challenges.
- Have a better idea about why advancing in life and success is important for you.
- Can perform better than other people.

It is only the start, though. There are various other perks that come along with this, along with having better health. Better health indicates that you can have more energy to do things and stay with all those people you care about.

Those with a growth mindset have higher chances of embracing challenges. Also, they can use feedback besides learning from mistakes and failures in place of dwelling on them. When you have a growth mindset, you can enjoy learning new things.

It can help you to be more creative as you are most likely to pursue solutions with persistence. When you focus on bettering yourself instead of protecting yourself, you will not feel threatened by the success and intelligence of others. You are most likely to admire other people, learn from them, and also find inspiration in success.

Developing a Growth Mindset for Freedom

Having a growth mindset can provide you more freedom so that you can attain your full potential and be in alignment with your values in place of being held by all sorts of limiting beliefs. With such kind of freedom, everything will seem possible for you.

As you get to experience this kind of freedom, you will start to believe that you have got the ability to alter not only your life but the lives of other people too. You will not regard anything to be static.

How to Develop a Growth Mindset?

Here are some of the ways in which you can develop a growth mindset easily.

Asking different questions

Questions can act as the building blocks of learning as you think of them. When you keep pushing yourself to try even harder next time, you will not be able to learn anything. In place of doing this, as you fail, try to reword your questions. Ask yourself, "What are the things that I can do differently?" or "What are the things that worked and what didn't?" Such a strategy can help you a lot so that you do not work hard and get the same results all the time.

Getting feedback proactively

The above-mentioned questions are surely a part of feedback; however, you can try to look for feedback in other ways all the time. Taking feedback positively will help you build new skills so that you can deal with the problems at hand in a better way the next time. Feedback acts as an important tool that can support growth. You will have to welcome feedback actively as feedback can make you reflect and provide you with ideas for adopting new behaviors and practices. Also, try to push yourself to provide constructive and honest feedback so that you can help other people learn and grow.

Focusing on personal improvement

Learning is more like a process. Having a growth mindset is not about embracing a challenge. It is about meeting it and welcoming the next challenge at the same time. It is all about learning, increasing skills and knowledge, and getting better constantly. But how is it possible to develop and maintain that focus on constant improvement?

The first thing that you will need to do is disassociate improvement from failure. You will have to stop thinking that "room for improvement" always indicates failure. Try to make a new goal the moment you accomplish a goal. You can never stop learning. People who possess a growth mindset are well aware of constantly creating new goals to keep themselves stimulated.

Taking ownership over your attitude

Try to own it as you display and act from a growth mindset. You will have to acknowledge yourself for the growth perspective and try to maintain the same as much as you can. However, always remember that your mindset can alter by the project, day, or skills involved. You will need to be mindful of triggers that tend to bring out old behaviors and patterns. For instance, seek out ways so that you can focus on learning more than social approval. As you try to prioritize approval more than learning, you will do nothing other than sacrifice your growth potential.

Celebrating growth with other people

When you appreciate the growth in a true sense, try to share your progress with friends, family, and coworkers. As you model growth mindset behaviors and discuss the same, it can help and encourage people around you to identify their potential. When they find you striving to improve yourself on a constant basis and celebrating the growth and success of others, it can foster a sense of teamwork. It will act like a genuine fellowship where people take an interest in the learning and development of each other. Additionally, try to be vulnerable when in the company of other people. Try to worry less and focus on experimenting more. It will help in making it easier for you to take risks in the future.

Trying out different learning tactics

When it comes to learning, there is no one-size-fits-all kind of model. All that can work for one person might not work for someone else. So, you can try out various kinds of tactics and determine the one that works the best for you. Try to learn from the mistakes of others.

It might not be that wise to compare yourself to other people all the time. But it is necessary to realize that we tend to share the same kind of weaknesses most often.

So, it is possible to learn from the strengths of others and also from their mistakes. You will have to seek out and appreciate different perspectives. Start conversations with groups and people that you might not engage with normally. You will need to approach such conversations with an open mind so that you can find out new perspectives.

Try to be open to seeing your views being challenged. When you get fresh insights, it can help in stimulating your creativity besides encouraging you to try out new strategies. Cultivate grit, and when you have a bit of extra determination, you will have higher chances of seeking approval from yourself instead of from other people.

Valuing the process over the end result

Never misunderstand this to mean that end results are of no importance. There is no doubt that end results are quite important as you opt for achieving a goal. But people with a growth mindset can also enjoy and value the overall learning process. Also, they never mind when it needs more effort and time than they anticipated initially. You will have to be aware and accept that learning takes time. Never expect to master anything within a span of a few hours. Keep in mind that growth holds more importance than speed. You will have to understand that learning fast is never the same as learning well. Also, learning well needs permitting time for mistakes.

Improving self-awareness

Knowing your strengths, tendencies, triggers, and yourself can play an essential role in developing and maintaining a growth mindset. You will have to try to discover and leverage your strengths. Always embrace and acknowledge imperfections. Trying to hide from your weaknesses indicates that you can never overcome them. Also, take out some time every day so that you can successfully reflect on your learning.

Viewing challenges as new opportunities

Whenever you decide to develop a growth mindset, you will need to learn to embrace all kinds of uncertainties. You will have to understand that for proper learning, you are required to be challenged. You will need to accept all those situations where you might seem to be weak so that you can relish all the opportunities for self-improvement. Try to opt for tough tasks and projects. Choose those things that will take you out of your comfort zone. Dedicate effort and time to master the same. The key here is to persist as you come across feedback – keep trying different approaches until you come across the one that works the best.

Upgrading vocabulary

You will need to upgrade your vocabulary. For instance, replace words like "failing" with the word "learning." As you fall short of any goal or make a mistake, you have not failed; you have learned new things. Just like how Thomas Edison said, "I haven't failed. I just found 10,000 ways that do not work." In the same way, use the word "yet." Whenever you tend to struggle with any work, keep in mind that you have not just mastered the same "yet."

Keeping in mind that the brain keeps evolving

Neither of our brains is fixed; our minds should not be either. There exists a close connection between "brain training" and learning. Just like the rest of the body, the brain also acts in the form of a muscle that is required to be worked out.

Similar to the way in which you can train the body to make it perfect and stronger for the physical feat, you can also train the brain and improve emotional reactions and cognitive skills. In this way, you will be able to reframe what you think is possible and inspire yourself to aim even higher.

Visualizing Your Future

Being able to reach your goals, specifically when they are lofty, is always a lot easier said than done. In any form, success takes a great deal of hard work along with planning. It is the reason why some dreams cannot be realized fully for years. But if you want to help yourself and see some actual progress, visualizing your future while you achieve your goals can make a huge difference. It does not indicate that this method will work like magic or success will be that simple. However, experts believe that visualization can help in getting your brain on the correct wavelength. It can help in setting things in motion. Here are some of the ways in which you can visualize your future in a better way.

Visualize your life once you get to achieve your goals

Regardless of the kind of goal, take your time to visualize what your life would look like as you achieve it. For instance, if your goal is to get a work promotion, visualize your boss calling you and informing you about the title change or the raise. Try to picture the extra salary going into your bank account or your new business cards. It is the ultimate outcome, and being able to picture it can provide you with a clear idea of the direction you are headed to.

Visualizing the steps you will take to get there

It can also help when you try to picture the process that you will have to go through to get to your destination. Try to imagine all the steps that are required to attain your goal. For instance, if you wish to be healthier, try to imagine yourself starting your day with a proper breakfast, taking vitamins, hitting the gym, eating balanced meals, and getting a good night's sleep. As you go through such small steps in mind, it will be a lot easier for you to add them to your routine.

Picturing everything in detail

Whether you are trying to picture an end result or the steps that you will have to take, it is necessary to envision it in as much detail as possible. Who is with you? What is the first thing they see as they look at you? What is your feeling? As you get up in the morning, what is the first clue that indicates things are different? Such things can serve as an incredible source of motivation.

Creating a vision board

Start collecting quotes and images that you think represent how you would want your future self to look. Then, develop a vision board and try to give it a proper place in your life. Try to hang it in a place where you can look at it all the time and study the board every day. As you do so, it will help in cementing your goals, trigger your inspirations, and get accountability to meet them.

Writing down all your goals

Writing down your goals will provide the same kind of effect if you feel that vision boards are not your thing. Also, it can help you determine the ones that might not work and remove the same. When you write down your goals, you can easily find out if they are attainable and reasonable. If they are, there is nothing to worry about, and you can move ahead with them. However, if they are not, never feel afraid to revise them.

Setting mini-goals along your way

It is quite an easy thing to get tripped on the way to achieving your goals, especially when you are not able to see quick success. So, you will plan for that moment in advance. Try to break your goals into smaller ones and concentrate on those. It can ensure victory in every step. None of us are fond of waiting too long to see the end results. So, when you get to celebrate the smaller victories, you can have an enhanced chance of getting to your end goal.

Putting in the work

It would have been great if all it needed was a moment's visualization, and in that way, your goals were realized. However, we all know that it will also need some honest hard work. Try to have a look at your timeline and the list of goals. Find out the next logical thing on the path and determine the steps you will require to take to move that one along. After that, just do it. Is there any need to take a class? Or change a habit? The answer is surely yes.

Exercise

Being able to visualize your future is not that tough. You can start by creating a list of goals that you have got in mind. After that, take each of your goals and try to note down the first thing that comes to your mind regarding the same. If it is something positive, you can surely move ahead with it and visualize the future of the goal in your life. If it is something negative, you will need to discard the goal.

Chapter 10: Learn to Love Yourself

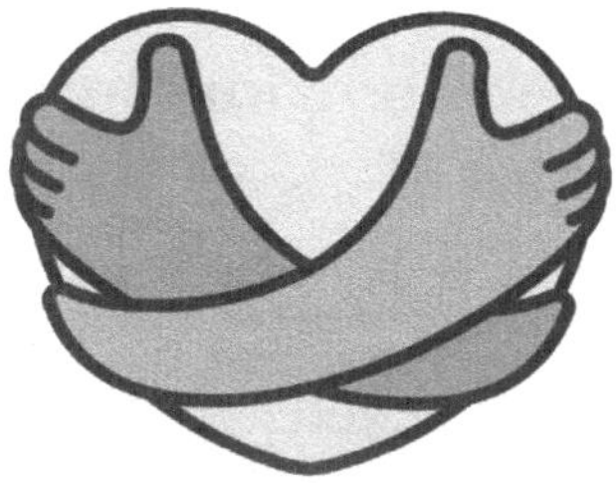

To love yourself is to experience security and happiness on a new level. Most of us tend to search for external love as that is how we found security and love in our childhood. We got rewarded with these things when we did something good. But we fail to grow out of this, and we keep looking for love from others. However, the love that we search for can only come from within. It is also why the love of someone else is not enough for you to truly feel happy. You can never feel safe when you cannot be comfortable with your capabilities. You will need to learn to love yourself with which you can push through your limiting beliefs and live a life that can truly shine.

Develop Self-Worth

Self-worth is the way you feel about yourself or the kind of opinion you hold about yourself. We all face times when we feel a bit low or find it tough to have faith in ourselves. But when this turns out to be a long-term situation, it might result in issues, including mental health problems like anxiety and depression. Some of your low self-worth symptoms could be the signs of these problems. Self-worth is the result of life experiences and especially what happened to us in our childhood. But keep in mind that you can develop your self-worth at any age. Here are some of the ways in which you can enhance your self-worth.

Identifying and challenging the negative beliefs

The first thing you will need to do is identify your negative beliefs regarding yourself and then challenge the same. Try to notice the thoughts that you get about yourself. For instance, you might think, "I have no friends" or "I am not capable enough to do that." As you have such thoughts, try to search for evidence that can contradict all those statements. Try to write down both evidence and statement, and keep looking back at it so that you can remind yourself that the negative thoughts you have about yourself are not true.

Identifying the positives about yourself

It can really help if you can write down positive things about yourself, like being good at sports or good things that others have said about you. The moment you tend to feel low, try to have a look back at all these things. You will have to remind yourself that there exists lots of good about you. Generally, positive internal dialogue can act as a great tool to improve self-esteem. In case you find yourself saying things such as, "I am a big failure" or "I am not good enough," you can turn things around by using your own statements. You can say, "I can be more confident by seeing myself in a more positive way," or "I can beat this."

Developing positive relationships and avoiding negative ones

You will surely find that there are certain relationships and people who can make you feel better about yourself compared to others. Also, there will be people who tend to make you feel bad about yourself. You will need to avoid such people as much as you can. You will have to develop a relationship with people who can make you feel great about yourself and stay away from the relationships that tend to drag you down.

Giving yourself a break

There is no need to be perfect every hour of the day. Also, there is no need to always feel good about yourself. Self-worth will vary from one situation to the other, from hour to hour, and day to day. There are people who feel positive and relaxed with coworkers and friends but shy and uneasy with new people. Others might be in command of themselves at work and struggle socially. No matter what is the case, you will have to give yourself a break. All of us have times when we feel down or find it tough to maintain self-belief.

The key here is not to be hard on yourself. You will need to be kind to yourself and not critical. Avoid comparing yourself to other people as it can reinforce all your negative views. In fact, it can give others a negative opinion about you. You can boost your self-worth any time by providing a treat to yourself whenever you succeed in doing anything.

Being more assertive and learning to say “no”

People who suffer from low self-worth are most likely to find it hard to stand up for themselves or simply say “no” to other people. It indicates that they might become over-burdened at work or home as they cannot refuse anyone. But what most people fail to realize is that it can increase stress besides making it harder to manage. So, it can be said that developing your assertiveness can help in improving your self-worth. At times, acting as if you have full belief in yourself can truly help in enhancing self-worth.

Develop Self-Image

Your self-image is the way in which you see yourself both externally and internally. Self-image influences how you see yourself, how you interact with other people, and how you feel about your surroundings. So, it can be said that your self-image has got some broad influence over your life. When you develop a positive self-image, it can help in boosting your mental, physical, emotional, spiritual, and social well-being. But a negative self-image can reduce your well-being in your overall life functioning and satisfaction.

Your self-image is by no means fixed. It can adapt and evolve as you grow as individuals and also through your interactions with other people. For example, as you practice certain abilities and skills and grow and learn, you will be more likely to see yourself as a competent and capable individual. Your self-image assesses this kind of info continuously and the kind of attitude you hold towards other people.

Also, it is not only the things that you do to yourself that can influence your self-image. It can also get influenced by your relationships and interactions with other people. For instance, if you interact with all those people regularly who are encouraging and supportive of you, you will have a higher chance of developing a positive self-image.

Such relationships can reinforce all those things you see while looking in the mirror, no matter if your view is distorted or not. Here are some of the ways in which you can develop your self-image.

Let loose and have fun

Keep in mind that you will only get one life to live. If you do it right, one will be good enough for you. All of us have heard of such things but never thought of them deeply. It is the perfect time to do that. As you are trying to do all those things that can help in changing your self-image, why not try to have fun while doing the same?

You can go all crazy and opt for all those things that you have wanted to do all the time. Keep ticking off things from your bucket list as you complete them. Doing so will help in instilling a never seen self-confidence in you. It is all that you want – a positive self-image filled with confidence. It will make you feel that you are a confident person who is never fearful of doing all those things he/she loves.

Create a list of life moments you are most proud of

It is another great exercise that can help you focus on all those things that you have achieved in life. At times, we just tend to forget how amazing we actually are as individuals. Preparing such a list can help you to remember all those things. The list can include things that are as big as winning competitions, achieving any high-level of accomplishment that you have been working on for a long time, or getting recognized for your contribution. You can also include small things like completing a task or learning to be more sociable. You can consider the way you have confronted barriers and challenges in your life and how your life skills have permitted you to deal with those things. The aim is to ensure that the proud life moments and achievements remind you of what you have offered to the world till now and all that you are capable of doing in the future.

Making a life-appreciation bank

The list that you will need to prepare in this exercise will be a lot bigger than the last two. The goal here is to develop an exhaustive and comprehensive list of all those things you are truly thankful for in life. Everyone will develop a unique list as we all have a different life and different things that we can be thankful for. As you are done with making your list, cut up each item and place them in any kind of container. Whenever you feel that you require a bit of self-image boost, you can go and grab one of these things from your life-appreciation bank and read them.

You get to decide how the rules work. For instance, after you are done reading an item from your bank, you can either remove it or just throw it back in the mix again. Or you might want to read two or three things at once. The rules are completely flexible, and it is all on you how you create them. The only thing that matters is that you end up with a bit of self-image boost that you desire.

Keep in mind that your self-image is nothing permanent. It is more like a dynamic concept that will keep varying as you evolve, grow, and also how you view yourself changes. So, never allow yourself to get stuck with a negative self-image.

Develop Self-Kindness

Instead of trying to change your deeply rooted values, you can start by lessening the kind of impact they gave to you by altering the way you see yourself. You can start to do this with self-kindness. Self-kindness is all about being kind, gentle, and understanding with your own self. It also involves accepting that no one can be perfect and understanding that there is always a potential for growth and learning in every mistake made by you. Here are some of the ways in which you can develop self-kindness.

Opt for a digital detox

Do you hold an unhealthy relationship with technology? The digital world has turned out to be a curse for some people besides being a gift for others. It is because it has both connected and disconnected us from one another and, most importantly, from ourselves.

So, a digital detox is a great way to come back to the current moment where real life exists. As you take away some time from social media, it can provide you more chances to spend time doing all those things you love. In fact, you will be able to reconnect with your own self. So, the next time you get the urge to get online, just step back and question yourself, "What is happening inside me at the moment that is triggering me to distract myself?"

Trying out new things

Routines are actually a great thing. However, the moment you get stuck in them, you will have fewer opportunities to try out new things. Can you recall the last time when you tried to get out of your comfort zone and did something that was not ordinary or regular for you?

The majority of people tend to get up at the same time every morning, have the same coffee, eat the same kind of breakfast, and work with the same group of people. There is nothing to wonder why people tend to feel stagnant in life. We have just settled for a life that is known as "sameness." If it turns out to be the way in which your life floats the boat, there is nothing wrong with it. But if you crave some energy and excitement, the time has come to change your game and opt for some new experiences. Always remember that the more you will try, the more will be your chances to develop newfound passions.

Expressing gratitude

Feeling gratitude is a powerful tool. Instead of continuously wishing for all those things that you do not have, there is always strength in appreciating what you have at the moment. You can either go for gratitude walks or prepare a gratitude journal. As you try to concentrate on your blessings, all you do is employ a gentle inner voice and simply shift the focus away from your shortcomings and externally to the world, with all the beauty.

Finding the right kind or level of generosity

There are three basic reciprocity styles – giver, taker, and matcher. Givers tend to be the most generous people, and we all know that generosity is a superb way of putting compassion into use. But givers can end up being both the most successful and least successful people. It is because they might fall into the pattern of selfless giving where they ignore all their needs. It can never be selfless when you want generosity to work for you for your well-being.

So, when you try to be generous, ensure that you are well aware of your requirements before you tend to progress. After that, choose the recipient of generosity consciously. You will also have to pay attention to available resources. Also, ensure that you enjoy it while being generous. Try to notice all the differences that you can make and never forget to give back to your own self.

Develop Self-Care

Self-care is not only about finding ways in which you can relax. It involves taking care of yourself physically, mentally, socially, emotionally, and spiritually. To take care of your well-being and health, it is necessary to strike a balance that will let you pay attention to each of the areas. At times, you might just need more self-care in one area to restore balance or in order to find relief from some sort of stress.

Social self-care

Socialization is one of the primary keys to self-care. However, it might be hard sometimes to make time for friends, and it is also quite easy to neglect your relationships as life gets busy. Keep in mind that close connections are necessary for well-being. One of the easiest ways to maintain as well as cultivate close connections is to dedicate energy along with time to developing relationships with other people. There are no fixed hours that anyone “should” dedicate to their friends or focus on their relationships. We all come with a bit varying social requirements. The primary key here is determining your social needs and then keeping aside time in your everyday schedule so that you can create an optimal social life.

Physical self-care

Keep in mind that you will always have to take care of your body properly when you want to work in an efficient way. Remember that there exists some deep relationship between the mind and body. As we care for the body, we can feel and think better. Taking care of your physical self involves the way in which you fuel your body, the amount of sleep you get, how well you care for your physical requirements, and how much physical activity you do. When you have a healthy body, you can also have a healthy mind.

Mental self-care

The things that you fill your mind with and how you think can easily affect your psychological health. Mental self-care involves all those aspects that can help in keeping your mind sharp, such as puzzles or learning a subject that truly fascinates you. Or you might find that watching movies or reading books helps in fueling your mind. It also includes doing all those stuff that can help in staying healthy mentally. For instance, being able to practice self-acceptance along with self-compassion can help in the maintenance of a healthy inner dialogue.

Spiritual self-care

It has been found that leading a lifestyle that includes spirituality is always a healthy lifestyle. However, being able to nurture your spirituality does not have to include religion. It can actually involve anything that can help in developing a sense of understanding, connection, or meaning with our universe. No matter if you love to attend religious services, praying, or meditate, self-care from the aspect of spirituality is necessary.

Emotional self-care

It is essential to develop healthy skills of coping so that you can take care of uncomfortable emotions, such as anger, sadness, and anxiety. Emotional self-care involves all those things that can help us express and acknowledge our feelings safely and regularly. Whether you talk to a close friend or your partner regarding how you feel or keep aside time to enjoy leisure activities that help in processing emotions, it is necessary to include emotional self-care in life.

Importance of self-care

Having a proper self-care routine can provide you with various kinds of essential health benefits. Some of them are:

- Reduces stress and improves resilience.
- Reduces depression and anxiety.
- Increases energy.
- Improves happiness.
- Strengthens interpersonal relationships.
- Reduces burnout.

Self-care is an important thing as it can help promote health, prevent diseases, and also helps in coping better with illness. As you prepare your self-care plan, the following steps can help you a lot.

- **Considering the stressors:** Think about all those areas that you think lead to stress and also think of ways in which you can address such stress.

- **Assessing your needs:** Try to prepare a list of various parts of your life along with major activities that you get involved in daily. Relationships, school, work, and family are some of the things that you can include in your list.

- **Taking small steps:** There is no need to tackle everything at once. Try to determine a small step that can be taken on your part to get started with taking care of yourself in a better way.

Develop Self-Compassion

Having self-compassion indicates being able to relate to yourself in a way that is accepting, forgiving, and loving when the situations are not optimal. Here are some of the ways in which you can nurture self-compassion.

Change your mindset

It might feel quite challenging at times to lift yourself up. However, when you desire to develop compassion for yourself, you will need to alter your mindset. Self-compassion can be started the moment you change your thoughts. For instance, you can focus on the fact that your behavior was bad and not you. As you learn to label behaviors, you can start being kinder to yourself and open your mind to the possibility that you can make changes.

Try mirroring positivity

In a study, the participants were asked to look in a mirror when they were asked questions like, "Can looking at the mirror be detrimental to your mental health?" You must have guessed it, but it was found that the participants experienced an increase in their levels of stress and anxiety as they stared in the mirror for about ten minutes.

A complete period of ten minutes is enough to provide anyone time to stress out every pore and causes self-critical talk to take charge. But the same thing can be reversed by repeating positive affirmations about yourself every time you see yourself in the mirror. With time, you will surely find yourself being more positive regarding your own image.

Finding common ground with other people

While the concept of self-compassion is all about how you care about yourself, a great way to develop it is to develop connections with other people. As you open yourself up to be with others, you will find that you are not alone. All of us struggle to treat ourselves with kindness at one point or the other. When you get to recognize this, it can make your struggles more manageable.

Paying attention to where your passion lies

We all are passionate about one thing or the other. You will surely have things that truly matter to you; your loved ones or a hobby. No matter what it is that gets you excited, let yourself concentrate on that. Try to do all that you need to spend more time enjoying it. Self-compassion is all about letting yourself be passionate without fear or shame.

Chapter 11: Make Self-Love a Priority

There is absolutely nothing wrong with putting energy into your relationships with loved ones. Or it is great to focus your attention on finding a new friend or a romantic partner. We all need intimacy, love, and companionship. So, you will be concentrating on yourself as you pursue all such needs.

It can also be said that when you do not tend to stop to consider others, your relationships will not thrive. But at the same time, trying to neglect your desires and dreams can easily hold you back.

When you live a life based on the pursuit of the happiness of other people, it will not bring you much joy. With time, you will start to feel drained. What to do here? You will need to pay attention to self-love. You will have to make self-love a priority in your life.

Getting Better Acquainted With Your Own Self

Developing a strong self-relationship can be a superb way to get back your focus to yourself. When you feel uncertain about your identity, it can make it hard to get clarity on all that you desire from life. Without any familiarity with who you are, you will not be able to do much to attain your goals, get your requirements met, or live according to your own values.

Any kind of significant event like a career change, breakup, personal crisis, or childbirth can prompt growth. It can also cast a light on the ways you have changed. Such kind of illumination might call into question all those things that you knew you were aware of yourself as new identity aspects emerge for the first time. You might not welcome this self-knowledge immediately, specifically when it contradicts the existing perception of the person you are.

However, not being able to acknowledge your growth can easily leave you feeling unfulfilled and incomplete. Such kind of uncertainty can start affecting your sense of self-worth, emotional well-being, and connection with other people. Trying to approach all such changes within yourself with curiosity can help you acclimate easily.

Making Sure You Seek What You Want

There are people who tend to care about the opinions of their loved ones. You might automatically not do everything that your friends or family suggest. However, you surely try to weigh their guidance carefully as you need to make any decision. It is quite helpful when you get insight from other people, especially when it comes to big decisions. But still, it is necessary to develop a distinction between determining value in this guidance and allowing it to sway you from the preferred course.

Such kind of a difference might get a little blurred at times. In fact, you might not be able to realize at first that the dreams you have are actually the dreams of someone else. For instance, you had a little bad luck with dating. Your friends and family try to reassure you that you will get the right person with time. They might even encourage you to keep trying. But it won't happen if you do not want it to.

Societal ideals around relationships and dating often tend to suggest that single people are incomplete and lonely. However, in reality, many people do find being single more fulfilling than opting for being in relationships that they do not want. So, when you discover that you have no interest in finding anyone, try to honor the truth.

Developing Self-Care Plan

Concentrating on yourself revolves around practices of self-care that can also meet your requirements. Self-care will let you turn your focus toward yourself in a proper way. Every human being has an array of basic needs that play an essential role in overall well-being, including physical exercise, nutrition, sleep, and relaxation.

In case you end up neglecting these, you will not be able to get enough time to recharge from the various sources of life stress. In fact, you might not be able to notice much impact at first. However, you will surely come across some unwanted alterations in your mental and physical health with time. In order to get started with your self-care plan:

- Add food items to your diet that can boost your mood.
- Take out time for physical activities.
- Draw or write in a mood journal.

- Try meditation.
- Set a target to spend two hours in nature every week.
- Read a book.

There is no need to opt for each of these. It would be wise of you to start small. Select one thing that you can work on and slowly work in the direction of all those practices that can make you feel good.

Staying Away from Comparison

The majority of people tend to compare themselves to other people. You might feel a little envious of a friend who seems to be happy all the time. You think, "If only I had their life, I would have been happy too." However, you might not be aware of how they actually found fulfillment in life. Even when happiness tends to stem from all those things they have, we all are different.

So, there is no guarantee that having the same things in life will deliver the same joy to you. Comparing yourself to another person might motivate you to opt for similar goals, such as your dream car, a nice house, or a romantic partner. That cannot be considered a bad thing as long as the new ideals you develop do not overshadow the existing values in your life.

Comparisons might turn out to be quite problematic the moment they start to distract you from all those things that matter to you in the true sense. As a result, you might end up working in the direction of something that you do not even want.

You do so as you believe it can help in resolving your dissatisfaction. In place of trying to compare yourself with other people, try to look at all those things that you already possess. What do you feel grateful for? What or who brings you joy? Where do you want to be in five years?

Examining Your Values

It is quite a common thing to lose sight of your values. It is especially the case when you find yourself on a hard path or find yourself single after an extensive period of being in a relationship. As you take time to reconsider all those values, it can help in refocusing your attention on the person you are or who you wish to be.

For instance, if you value your community, you can look for ways in which you can share resources or time with your community. When you get to identify your values, you can start to find ways in which you can include them in your path of life in a meaningful way. Certain values, like optimism, bravery, or being adventurous, might come to you naturally. Other values, like accountability, leadership, or honesty, might need a bit of work from your side. But as you start to live your life according to your values, it can help in increasing life satisfaction besides improving mental health.

Tips to Make Self-Love a Priority

Here are some tips that can help you in making self-love a priority.

- **Taking back your charge:** You will have to suppress the victim mentality and try to take charge of your life. There is no benefit in pointing fingers at other people or trying to blame the circumstances. It is now time to own up and take back the control. The moment you can take ownership of your life is when you can get back the power to change.

- **Letting go:** Try to let go of all those things that are not serving you any good. It also includes friendships, relationships, habits, and so on. The aim is to get rid of all those things that might hold you back. Doing so might trigger feelings of loneliness. However, give it time, and it will pass. Replace destructive thoughts with good habits, toxic people with good ones, and so on.

- **Committing:** You will need to be 110% committed to your self-love journey. There should be no excuses at all. Never allow anything to get in the way of you and your self-relationship.

Exercise

Being able to set self-love as a priority depends on you. It is you who can decide what amount of time to dedicate to which things. Try to set aside about half an hour every day for self-love. It might not be easy at first, but try to manage five minutes a day and slowly increase that to thirty minutes.

Chapter 12: Importance of Social Support System in Life

Most people might not be aware of this, but it is necessary to have a proper system of social support in life. Social support is considered the key aspect of strong psychological health along with solid relationships. Generally, social support includes developing friends and family networks that you can opt for when in need. No matter if you deal with a personal problem and require instant help or just desire to enjoy some time with all those who genuinely think of you, all such relationships work as an important part of the way you lead your everyday life.

Keep in mind that social support is the only thing that builds up people during stress and provides the strength necessary to move ahead in life. However, social support cannot be regarded as a one-way street. Along with depending on other people, you also need to play the part of support for the same individuals in life.

Why Is Social Support Necessary?

Mental health professionals or psychologists often discuss the necessity of developing a proper network of social support. As you try to attain your goals or cope with any sort of crisis, professionals suggest taking the support of your family and friends. Nothing can be stronger than social support. It has also been found that there exists some connection between social relationships and various forms of wellness and health. A bad form of social support might lead to loneliness and depression.

In fact, it might result in altering brain functioning besides increasing the risks of:

- Depression
- Alcohol usage
- Suicide
- Cardiovascular diseases

A study involving middle-aged men found that all those who have strong emotional and social support are less likely to die compared to the ones who fail to develop such relationships. So, what are your social environment aspects that are so important for your health? Can your social environment impact your well-being? There exist two important facets of the social world which tend to contribute to our health. They are social integration and support.

Social Support

It indicates the material along with psychological resources delivered by some strong social networks to support us deal with stress. Social support of this kind might be seen in various forms. They might involve:

- Giving advice to some close friends as they deal with a tough situation.

- Helping an individual with multiple everyday tasks when they feel sick or supporting financially when in need.

- Providing empathy, caring, and concern to close people in need.

Social Integration

It involves participating in several kinds of social relationships that range from friendships to partnerships. It involves intimacy, emotions, along with some sense of acceptance in various social groups while also participating in:

- Partnership
- Family
- Social activity
- Religious communities

It is suggested by experts that taking part in such kinds of social relationships can confer some sort of protective benefit against damaging health consequences.

Social Support and Its Types

Supportive networks might be seen in various structures and play varying parts in our lives.

Emotional support

At times, you can get emotional support from the individuals in your life. When you require it, they back you up. Also, when you want to cry, when anything fails to go your way, they are there for you. Such kind of help could turn out to be specifically essential at times when people tend to feel lonely or stressed.

Instrumental support

You can get instrumental support from all those who are a part of your social network. Such people tend to provide you with a helping hand any time you require it and look after your physical requirements. It can include providing you a ride at times as your car is in the service center or providing you a great hot meal as you fall ill. Such kind of support is necessary when we have instant requirements that are required to be taken care of.

Informational support

Your social network could also deliver you what is called informational support. It might include supplying advice, guidance, mentoring, and information. Support of this kind can turn out to be quite necessary as you make big decisions. Or when you decide to bring new things into life. When you get such kind of support, you can be less stressed out or anxious regarding the issues that you are fighting to deal with. It is all because of the advice of a mentor, trusted friend, or loved one.

As you can think, individuals who are a part of your social support network can take on various roles.

For instance, a teacher can provide you with informational support, while your parents can provide you with all kinds of support. When you develop and possess a strong network of social support, you will surely get the kind of help when you truly require it.

Health Benefits

As now you are aware of your social support system and that it involves various kinds of social support and integration, let's look at how it can influence both mental and physical health.

Behaviors and health choices

Being a participant in social groups tends to have some sort of normative influence on attitudes, often having some influence on whether people exercise, opt for healthy diets, drink, smoke, or resort to illegal substances. Social support might result in negative influence at times like this when influence or peer pressure results in dangerous or poor choices regarding health.

But support and pressure from a group can also result in making people opt for healthy behaviors too. You can realize how essential social support could be in case you have ever given it a try to get rid of any bad habit, like smoking. When social support fails to support you, it could make your success look harder. But when family and friends provide you with encouragement and support, achieving tough goals will seem easier.

Dealing with stress

Social support can aid in dealing with stress. It has been proven that stress can impart serious health consequences that range from increased risk of heart diseases to reduced immunity. When you stay surrounded by people who support and care for you, it can help you in coping with life stresses. The consequences of trauma-induced disorders, along with PTSD at the time of crisis, can be reduced with the help of social support.

Enhances motivation

Social relationships can help you in staying motivated when you try to attain your goals. For instance, people who try to quit smoking or lose weight often find that it helps to a great degree to connect with all those who are trying to achieve the same goals. As you talk to people who are experiencing the same kind of situation or problem can often turn out to be a source of empathy, motivation, and support.

As already said earlier, support is like a two-way street. When you get to identify the primary supporters in life, you will have to give your best so that you can develop those relationships. Try to connect with them daily and keep them updated regarding what is happening in your life. Explain your reasoning and invite them into your decisions. You will need to ask for their honest opinion.

Also, be open to feedback even when it is not what you hear all the time. The best supporters in your life will tell you the tough truths all the time and can help you see all your options from various perspectives. It is necessary to be open to advice. Your system of support will not be able to help you unless you can consider all that they have to say. As you make big decisions, discuss with the members of your support system who have got some knowledge in all those areas that you are not familiar with.

For instance, if you think about making some sort of substantial financial purchase, you will have to get in touch with someone who is an expert in matters of finance. All of us have got unique knowledge based on the experiences of our lives. You can use your support group knowledge to opt for the best decisions. That is the primary reason why you should always work to determine people in your life who can support you and concentrate on strengthening all those relationships. It can be beneficial to assess your relationships every once in a while.

- Would you be able to benefit from deepening the present relationships?

- Have you got enough social support?

- Could you opt for new social outlets?

You can make up your mind to be more proactive regarding getting and giving social support. It will only improve your life in a great way. If you struggle to make new friends or retain them, you can take the help of a therapist. They can assist you in the healthy management of your relationships so that you get the social support that you require to be the best.

Stop Waiting for the Outcome and Enjoy the Journey

It is quite easy to think that all you need to attain extraordinary success in life is to concentrate on results and use them to measure your progress. But such kind of a principle application is far away from being optimal. There is a lot more to success than just looking at the outcome without being able to understand that at the end of the day, it all comes down to your consistency. It also includes the process that is involved in completing the work. As you learn to concentrate your energy less on the outcomes and more on the techniques or processes, you can learn faster, be more successful, and be happier. Altogether you will be able to gain more in life as you pay attention to the process instead of the results. We human beings are never satisfied with the current circumstances. We have wants and needs that tend to be endless, and we have got the immense pressure of attaining results hovering over us all the time.

Most of us believe that it is only through results that we can secure our pathway for a better future. However, such kinds of thoughts can be overwhelming and selfish. It is especially the case when we consider that it stems from concerning ourselves with what other people think of us instead of what we need to think of ourselves. People who concentrate on the process instead of the results can always get a lot more in life. Here are some of the reasons why you can be a lot happier when you focus on the process instead of the results.

You can handle mistakes

Mistakes can be regarded as a part of existence, and none of us is perfect. Mistakes can help you grow and learn in life. As you concentrate on a specific desired outcome, you will be less willing to take risks or experiment.

You can gain satisfaction in your pursuit

Success is more like a journey than a destination. As you get focused on the process, you can be excited about being in the present moment and enjoying it fully. You can stay engaged, and you might also desire to dip deep into those avenues and opportunities. It is because it is all about gaining experience and learning faster at the end of the day.

You will have fewer distractions

Let us face it – there exists pressure when it is about delivering results. You want to prove a point, and you are all set to cut corners if you need to just to attain the results. When you try to focus your attention on the process, you will be able to cut off the noise of external factors. There will be less pressure. It is not about losing or winning. It is about gaining mastery in anything that you desire to pursue. You will not get disturbed. Keep in mind that it is not about satisfying the external factors. It is about conquering yourself.

You can be in charge

As you concentrate on the outcome, it will provide you partial control of whether you can reach it or not. There will be things that will keep working against you – health, time, competition, support group, and so on. The list is never-ending. You only need to deliver. However, you will develop internal control when you do not have the hovering challenge of obtaining results. It will result in higher empowerment, self-esteem, and in the end, great success. It will offer you a more meaningful life.

You can derive happiness from giving your best

There is great happiness in enjoying the fruit of your labor. That is the primary thing concentrating on the process can provide you. Things in your life might not always be the way you want them to be. But you can be happy that you dedicated yourself completely to the process and won internally. There is no benefit in trying to predicate your success on a certain result or outcome. It will only result in disappointment and frustration. Instead of permitting your happiness to be dependent on you attaining a certain result, allow your happiness to rely on how much you have worked to attain your goal.

Conclusion

Thank you for making it through to the end of this book; let's hope it was informative and was able to provide you with all of the tools you need to achieve your goals, whatever they may be.

Nothing in this world can be greater than self-love. Unless and until you can love yourself, the love of other people won't matter to you in life. Accept it instead of running away from it even when you feel stuck somewhere. If you try to run away, it will keep following you till the last day of your life, eating away your happiness. Cry, scream, or kick. Try to experience the awfulness of constant pain, but do not ignore it. Trying to stuff down all your pain inside yourself will make things complicated.

Self-love comes above everything else. To be more precise, concentrate on yourself above everything else. There won't be anything unless you can be there. Try to take out time for yourself. Be with yourself. Listen to what your heart has to say. Doing so will make your life wonderful besides bringing more happiness in life. Do not think of what others have got to say. Do only those things that feel right to you. Self-love is not an easy thing. It will take time, but your life will change forever once you can grab the idea.

Finally, if you found this book useful in any way, a review on Amazon is always appreciated!

9 789356 559660

Printed at Repro India Ltd.